SUPERCARS

DRIVING THE DREAM

Adam Phillips

igloo

This edition published 2006

First published in 2005
by Igloo Books Ltd
Cottage Farm,
Sywell,
NN6 OBJ
www.igloo-books.com

ISBN 1-84561-254-X

Project management: Kandour Ltd
Editorial and design management: Emma Hayley and Jenny Ross
Author and project co-ordinator: Adam Phillips
Design and layout: Kurt Young
Cover design: Kurt Young
Cover pictures contributed by Evo magazine
Pictures contributed by Evo magazine, Ford Motor Company Ltd,
Bugatti Automobiles S.A.S, Aston Martin, Koenigsegg Automotive AB,
Mitsubishi Motors Ltd, Ariel Motor Company Ltd
Printed in China

Contents

Introduction	4	Ferrari Enzo	48
The History Of The Supercar	6	Ferrari F430	54
Mercedes 300SL	8	Ford GT	60
Ford GT40	9	Honda NSX	68
Lamborghini Muira	10	Koenigsegg CC	74
Lamborghini Countach	11	Lamborghini Murcielago	80
BMW M1	12	Lamborghini Gallardo	86
Lotus Turbo Esprit	13	Maserati MC12	92
Ferrari 288 GTO	14	Mercedes-Benz McLaren SLR	98
Ferrari Testarossa	14	Mitsubishi Lancer Evolution VIII	104
Porsche 959	15	Pagani Zonda	110
Ferrari F40	15	Porsche Carrera GT	116
Bugatti EB110	16	TVR Sagaris	124
Jaguar XJ220	17	TVR Tuscan 2	130
McLaren F1	18	Future Perfect?	136
Ferrari F50	19	Bugatti Veyron	138
The Modern Supercar	20	Supercars On A Budget	142
Aston Martin Vanquish S	22	Ariel Atom 2	144
Aston Martin DB9	28	Lotus Exige	148
Aston Martin DBR9	34	Mercedes-Benz SLK350	152
Aston Martin V8 Vantage	36	Vauxhall VX220 Turbo	156
B Engineering Edonis	42		

What makes someone want to buy a car that costs a small fortune? Or a very large one for that matter? Surely a nice little Japanese hatchback with a 1.4-liter engine will do the job. After all, you don't need 1,000bhp to pop down to the local shopping mall or to pick up the kids from school. But that's missing the point–us humans have a passion for pushing forward; for wanting to outdo and challenge ourselves, and supercars are one of the ultimate expressions of this desire. And people will always want to buy into that.

Naturally, there are those that merely want a supercar as a trophy; to be driven once in a while to impress their peers and to show the world that their bank balance is in fighting form. Equally, there are those who understand that only the best will do; who want to experience the sensation and thrill of cars designed for pure driver indulgence. And if we can't afford them, then we want to respect and admire the creativity and engineering that has made the supercar what it is today.

After all, the early days of supercar development were heady ones–bold but small steps into the future where one supercar would offer the greatest performance while the other would deliver the best driving experience. And now the fruits of all that blood, sweat and tears over the past five decades are seemingly reaching their peak. From Britain and Italy through to America and Japan, the combined genius of designers and engineers has seen the supercars of today blend so many elements perfectly.

And they have to–we're a demanding bunch after all. We want those looks–the ones that linger in the mind well after glimpsing that exotic machinery for the first time. We want to know about the performance–the kind that defies belief when first scanning down a supercar's specifications. And we want the handling–the kind that offers huge grip, accessibility and feedback. Yes, we're a greedy bunch.

Modern supercars offer the best of all worlds (well, apart from the miles-per-gallon and luggage space that is)–and this book is a tribute to them. From supercars on a budget to exotica that can cost you a cool million, the automotive art featured in these pages show that we're all still as passionate about progress, and going fast, as we ever were.

The only question remaining is–if this is as good as it gets now, just what will be rolling down our roads in the future? We can't wait. Can you?

The History of the Supercar

There has never been a better time than now for supercar aficionados to indulge in their passion for automobile excellence. However, it has taken over 50 years of cumulative development and hard work by the world's greatest designers and engineers to bring us up to the modern day. Here we present some of the highlights of the supercar's emergence since its birth in the 1950s.

Mercedes 300SL
Gullwing
(1954–1957)

This is not a true supercar, but it is one that showed the way forward because of its incredible technology and performance; the 3-liter engine, producing 240bhp, could make the sprint from 0-60 in 8.8secs and hit a top speed of 145mph.

Innovations in technology saw the 300SL become the first ever production car to have fuel injection, and the car featured a space-frame chassis which, because of the chassis running down either side of the car, meant the 300SL had to have those now-famous gullwing doors. Furthermore, the 300SL also happens to be one of the most beautiful cars ever made–very much a supercar then.

Specifications:

Engine	2996cc
Max power	240bhp at 6,100rpm
Max torque	217lb ft at 4,800rpm
0-60mph	8.8secs
Top speed	135mph +

Ford GT40 MkIII (1967)

Ford's race car version of the GT40 humiliated Ferrari at Le Mans in the latter half of the 1960s (see page 60). It also spawned a road-going version in 1967 that was panned by critics for its sloppy road manners. But real drivers didn't care about its manners, because the GT40 MkIII could see off its competitors in a straight line with the 306bhp produced by its 4.7-liter V8 engine–and boasted 0-60 in 5.5secs. Its top speed of 170mph also hinted at what the future held for true supercars. Only seven GT40s (MkIII) were ever built.

Specifications:	
Engine	4736cc
Max power	306bhp at 6,000rpm
Max torque	229lb ft at 4,200rpm
0-60mph	5.5secs
Top speed	170mph

Lamborghini Muira (1966–1972)

Unveiled to a stunned audience at the Geneva Motor Show, Switzerland, in 1966, the Muira is what many believe to be the planet's first true supercar, partly because its mid-mounted engine was a world first. Just as importantly, the engine's placement had a direct effect on the car's appearance–and those looks are still stunning. The greatest version of Muira is the SV produced at the beginning of the 1970s, which saw the original's 350bhp increased to 385bhp. The only problem with the Muira is that the front end is prone to lift at high speeds because of the engine layout–so handle with care.

Lamborghini Muira SV specifications (1971–1972):

Engine	3929cc
Max power	385bhp at 7,850rpm
Max torque	294lb ft at 5,750rpm
0-60mph	6.0secs
Top speed	180mph

Other key cars from the 1960s:
Jaguar E-Type, Ferrari 275 GTB, Ferrari 365 GTB Daytona, Corvette Sting Ray, De Tomaso Mangusta.

Lamborghini Countach 25th Anniversary (1989–1990)

Lamborghini Countach (1974–1990)

It's one of the defining shapes in car history–the prototype Countach, which was shown for the first time in 1971, was greeted with rapture by the crowds. The replacement for the Muira, the sleek, sensual lines had been supplanted with dramatic lines and a wedge shape that would come to dominate the supercar world for the next ten years. The first Lamborghini Countach to be released (the LP400) featured a 3.9-liter V12 engine that could make the sprint from 0-60 in 5.6secs. Several incarnations of the Countach, which included the celebrated 5-liter Countach QV in 1985, followed over its illustrious 17-year reign as the king of the supercars. It has to be said though that the Countach represents the ultimate old-school supercar–it offered a driving experience that had to be learned; simply getting behind the wheel and flooring it was not to be recommended. After all, you can't tame a bull.

LP400 specifications (1974–1982):	
Engine	3929cc
Max power	375bhp at 8,000rpm
Max torque	268lbft at 5,000rpm
0-60mph	5.6secs
Top speed	180mph +

BMW M1
(1978–1981)

The M1 is one of the unsung heroes of the 1970s. It was BMW's first (and, so far, only) foray into creating a mid-engined supercar, and it could have worked out if the project hadn't been besieged by problems. It was intended that the M1 would be styled and built by Lamborghini, but because the raging bull was experiencing money woes, Bauer, in Germany, produced the car for BMW. More trouble was to strike–the car had been intended for the track but these plans fell through. It's a tragedy because the road-going M1 put the wind up its Italian rivals by offering the same levels of grip but pairing it with forgiving handling and bullet-proof reliability–not exactly a forte of Italian supercars at the time.

Specifications:

Engine	3453cc
Max power	277bhp at 6,500rpm
Max torque	243lb ft at 5,000rpm
0-60mph	5.6secs
Top speed	162mph

Other key cars from the 1970s: Maserati Bora, Porsche 911 2.7 RS, Porsche 911 Turbo, Aston Martin V8 Vantage.

Lotus Turbo Esprit SE (1989)

Lotus Turbo Esprit (1980–1992)

The Lotus Esprit has had a long and illustrious history dating back to when the car was first introduced in 1976. One of the most revered versions was the Turbo that first surfaced in 1980 and featured a four-cylinder aluminum engine that could produce 210bhp. The Esprit's 'credentials' were further increased thanks to a movie appearance–the Turbo was James Bond's vehicle of choice (both on the road and underwater) in *The Spy Who Loved Me*. Over the decades there have been numerous incarnations of the Esprit, but its production run (that spanned an incredible 28 years) came to a close on February 21st, 2004. Fans needn't worry though–Lotus are already designing its replacement.

Specifications:

Engine	2174cc
Max power	210bhp at 6,250rpm
Max torque	200lb ft at 4,500rpm
0-60mph	5.6secs
Top speed	150mph

Ferrari 288 GTO (1984–1985)

The mid-engined GTO is actually the forefather of the classic F40, but this 1980s supercar has earned its rightful place in the history books because its body was manufactured from composite materials such as carbon fiber – making it one of the very few cars to feature such race-developed technology. These lightweight materials coupled with a twin-turbo 2.8-liter V8 engine meant that the GTO was an extremely quick car with handling that was, let's just say, best exploited by the 'experienced driver'.

Specifications:

Engine	2855cc
Max power	400bhp at 7,000rpm
Max torque	466lb ft at 3,800rpm
0-60mph	4.7secs
Top speed	188mph

Ferrari Testarossa (1984–1992)

Aimed at being more of a GT than a hardcore road racer, the Testarossa ('Red Head') showed Ferrari heading in a more refined direction while retaining the astonishing speed and acceleration that all supercar owners demand. And the flat-12 engine saw to that with its 390bhp.

Specifications:

Engine	4942cc
Max power	390bhp at 6,300rpm
Max torque	354lb ft at 4,500rpm
0-60mph	5.3secs
Top speed	180mph

Porsche 959 (1987-1991)

Trust Porsche to come up with a world-class supercar–the 959 was able to hit 0-60 in under 4secs. This phenomenal acceleration was achieved with typical German efficiency using a rear-mounted twin-turbo flat-six engine that produced 450bhp. To get such power down onto the road, the 959 featured four-wheel drive paired with a six-speed gearbox, and the kind of stability needed to hit a cool 197mph.

Specifications:

Engine	2850cc
Max power	450bhp at 6,500rpm
Max torque	369lb ft at 5,000rpm
0-60mph	3.6secs
Top speed	197mph

Other key cars from the 1980s:
Aston Martin Bulldog, Aston Martin
Vantage Zagato, Ruf CTR Yellowbird.

Ferrari F40 (1987-1992)

Released to celebrate the company's 40th anniversary, the F40 was the last road car that the marque's creator, Enzo Ferrari, commissioned before he passed away–but what a swansong. It looked more like a race car than a supercar and it featured a 2.9-liter V8 engine that would see a brave driver propelled to over 200mph. The car is, of course, not for the faint-hearted but its position as one of the iconic supercars of any age is indisputable.

Specifications:

Engine	2936cc
Max power	478bhp at 7,000rpm
Max torque	425lb ft at 4,000rpm
0-60mph	3.9secs
Top speed	201mph

Bugatti EB110
(1992–1995)

It was supposed to be the rebirth of the Bugatti brand and, at first, the future was looking bright for the marque. While the EB110's looks may have been controversial, the Bugatti was a true supercar with staggering performance; it featured, thanks to the chassis and four-wheel drive, a colossal amount of grip to make the most out of all that power. Two versions were available–the 'humble' GT with 553bhp and the Supersport which boasted 603bhp. But alas, the Bugatti dream imploded in 1995 when the company went bust, mainly because of the global recession.

EB110 Supersport specifications:

Engine	3500cc
Max power	603bhp at 8,250rpm
Max torque	479lb ft at 4,250rpm
0-60mph	3.1secs
Top speed	218mph

Jaguar XJ220 (1992–1994)

Quite frankly, the Jaguar supercar was something of a debacle. Back in 1988 customers were bedazzled by promises of a huge V12 engine, coupled with a four-wheel drive, when the XJ220 prototype was unveiled. Down went the deposits as (very rich) people waited for the car's arrival in 1992. The trouble was that Jaguar replaced the engine with a V6 and dumped the four-wheel drive. Some angry customers withdrew their orders and demanded their deposits back; legal wranglings ensued. Add to this a world recession, and Jaguar's supercar foundered. The sad fact is that on its release, the XJ220 was still a fantastically fast car boasting supreme handling (in the dry)–and then there were those striking looks.

Specifications

Engine	2498cc
Max power	542bhp at 6,500rpm
Max torque	472lb ft at 5,000rpm
0-60mph	3.6secs
Top speed	210mph +

*McLaren F1
(1993–1997)*

Until recently, the McLaren F1 was the fastest car on the planet. Its BMW 6.1-liter V12 engine produced a staggering 627bhp and could propel the car up to 240mph. And never mind the 0-60 time–the F1 could hit 100mph in just 6.3secs. The key to the McLaren's success was the fact it was created entirely from carbon fiber and built on a philosophy that demanded it be put together with absolute precision. The resulting car can seat three people–the driver in the middle with two passengers to the side and back of him. The McLaren's production came to an end when customers decided that the price tag of £635,000/US$1,000,000 was perhaps stretching even them a little too much. The McLaren would also carve out a name for itself on the track by winning the Le Mans 24-hour race in 1995. The F1 then remains the supercar that all others are judged by.

Specifications:

Engine	6064cc
Max power	627bhp at 7,400rpm
Max torque	479lb ft at 4,000rpm
0-60mph	3.2secs
Top speed	240mph

Ferrari F50 (1995–1997)

What happens when you put a Formula One engine into a production car? Well, trust Ferrari to be the ones bold enough to try it–and, of course, to get it right with the F50. The 4.7-liter V12 lump featured in the supercar was a direct descendant of the engine that nearly earned Alain Prost top honours in the 1990 F1 World Championship. Just as important to the F50's achievement as a true race car made for the road was its easy-to-access driving experience– the F50 left its forefather the F40 for dead on a twisty track, so sweet and accessible was its handling. Perhaps the car's ungainly looks and zero practicality were the only thorns in its side–but those issues apart, the F50 was yet another classic Italian stallion from the Ferrari stables.

Specifications:

Engine	4698cc
Max power	513bhp at 8,000rpm
Max torque	347lb ft at 6,500rpm
0-60mph	3.7secs
Top speed	202mph

Other key cars from the 1990s:
Lamborghini Diablo, Chevrolet Corvette ZR1,
Dodge Viper, Ferrari F355, Ferrari 456,
BMW M5, TVR Cerbera, Porsche 993 GT2,
Subaru Impreza Turbo.

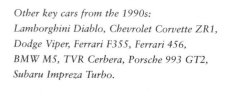

The Modern Supercar

Here is the culmination of what the best minds in the
supercar business have to offer thanks to the last 50 years.
From GTs through to roadsters, all the supercars
featured here offer the true car-lover a wealth of treasures
to indulge themselves in; looks that are intoxicating;
performance that is G-force defying; and a driving experience
that is truly unforgettable. Welcome to the state-of-the-
supercar-art...

The arrival of the original Vanquish and this, its more powerful brother the Vanquish S, has ushered in a new era for Britain's most iconic sports car company...

When Aston Martin unveiled the Vanquish in 2001, first impressions had to count–after all, here was a car that needed to make an impact. The Ford-owned company was coming out of the recession-ridden 1990s and needed an all-new flagship car to show the world that they were more than their classic DB7 coupe. Thanks to Ford's vision for the company and car designer maestro Ian Callum, the Vanquish hit its mark. Jaws dropped to the floor when the car was first shown–the Vanquish was that striking; that poised; that menacing; that... British.

Aston Martin Vanquish S

Featuring a V12 6-liter engine pumping out 460bhp, those bold good looks were backed up with an equally impressive driving experience– supremely comfortable on long cruises while being able to kick up its heels on the twisty stuff. Any concerns about the future of Britain's premier car brand had been well and truly kicked into touch.

Another key element of the Vanquish's success story was the way it was built. Ford wanted Aston Martin to become the home of new car technology–the Vanquish featured a body combining both aluminum and carbon fiber, which was lightweight enough to put itself in range of serious supercar territory.

But the car marque's crowning glory is the Vanquish S. The S came into existence to push the car further into Ferrari territory, and to appeal to the driver looking for a car that combines handcrafted tradition with the latest innovations from the world of Formula One and aerospace technology.

Debuted at the Paris Motor Show, France, in 2004, the S is the fastest production model Aston Martin has ever made. The 48-valve V12 6-liter engine now produces 520bhp over the previous Vanquish's 460bhp, and it can top 200mph. The S also features stiffer springs and dampers, plus shorter steering arms to give drivers the ultimate handling package.

As the flagship for Aston Martin, the Vanquish S is a true GT cruiser able to devour continents in style and comfort. Some nitpickers might argue that it's not a supercar in the strictest sense of the word, but with the Vanquish S's intoxicating mix of power and grace, it's the only word suitable to sum up its incredible talents.

"The Vanquish S is the fastest production model
Aston Martin has ever made"

From Start To Finish

It takes 396 hours for Aston Martin's engineers at the Newport Pagnall factory, in the UK, to hand-build the Vanquish S; the interior alone takes more than 70 hours to craft, and features eight hides of leather.

Nip And Tuck

Cosmetically the S has been given subtle tweaks over the original Vanquish; as well as changes to the car's nose, it has also a raised lip on the trunk to aid stability and balance while reducing lift.

What Lies Beneath

The Vanquish was always intended to show off Aston Martin as a hotbed of cutting edge technology. This is perfectly reflected by the materials that make up the car—aluminum is used for the bulkheads and floor while the windshield pillars and center tunnel are made from carbon fiber.

Something Old, Something New

Designed by car industry legend Ian Callum, the Vanquish manages to blend perfectly the old and the new into a modern and fresh look. Callum is reported to have said that it was the DB4 GT Zagato from the 1960s that fuelled his vision for the Vanquish.

Well Engineered?

For the original Vanquish launched in 2001, Aston put 50 prototypes through hellish tests across several continents to nail reliability—and managed to clock up an impressive 1,000,000 miles between them in the process.

Copyright Aston Martin

Copyright Aston Martin

Copyright Aston Martin

Aston Martin Vanquish S: The Specifications

Engine	Fuel injected 48-valve V12	0–60mph	4.7secs	Brakes Rear	Ventilated & grooved with four callipers/330mm/13in	Kerb Weight	1875kg/4134lbs
Valvetrain	DOHC 4 valves / cyl	0–100mph	9.8secs			Length	4665mm/184in
Displacement	5935cc	Maximum Speed	200mph +	Suspension Front	Double wishbones with monutube dampers, coil springs & anti-roll bar	Width	1923mm/76in
Maximum Power	520bhp at 7,000rpm	Steering	Rack and pinion with variable power assist			Height	1318mm/52in
Maximum Torque	425lb ft at 5,800rpm			Suspension Rear	Double wishbones with monutube dampers, coil springs & anti-roll bar	Wheels Front	9 x 19in
Transmission	Six-speed manual with paddle shifting	Brakes Front	Ventilated & grooved with six callipers/378mm/15in			Wheel Rear	10 x 19in
						Price	£174,000/US$255,000

While the Vanquish showed the world where Aston Martin's future lay, it's the DB9 that has further secured their place as one of the most desirable brands on the planet...

Any car enthusiast knows that the DB7 was an iconic British car, and one of the most beautiful in the world. The problem was that the DB7 had been around for a while and was beginning to show its age. It needed an all-new replacement–something that would put the wind up Ferrari and Porsche; while the Vanquish (see page 22) demonstrated that Aston had its eye firmly on the future, they still needed a lower priced car that would help the company shift 5,000 cars a year. The DB9 is that car–built at Aston Martin's all-new factory in Gaydon, UK, it is regarded as one of the greatest GTs ever built.

Aston Martin
DB9

Seeing it in the flesh for the first time with its low, sleek and muscular looks is enough to make you want to sign on the dotted line there and then. Those looks can be credited to design maestro Ian Callum who handed over the baton to Henrik Fisker to complete what many argue is the most beautiful car on sale today. But the DB9's beauty isn't merely skin deep–under the exterior is a wholly new platform.

Named the VH (Vertical and Horizontal), it's constructed from aluminum, and all the major mechanical and body components have been engineered from aluminum, magnesium or lightweight composite materials. This means that with its V12 450bhp engine, the DB9 is able to propel itself at a fierce pace on the straights because of its relative lightness but also to corner confidently because of its rigidity. Most importantly, the driver never feels left out, or scared, by the DB9.

While some supercars can feel like they'll make for the nearest hedge if you show them a moment's lack of concentration, the DB9 is renowned for its user-friendliness and its approachable and exploitable driving experience. This accessibility is easily managed by either a manual six-speed gearbox or a six-speed ZF automatic with paddle shifts that, while shaving 0.2secs off the car's 0–60 time, is highly regarded for its suppleness and smoothness.

The DB9's interior is more than a match for its elegant exterior–like any supercar should, it makes you feel special but let's face it, no one does leather and wood like Aston, and the DB9 is no exception with its elegant and seductive blend of materials.

While its predecessor the DB7 will always hold a special place in the history of the supercar–and be credited as the product that was key to Aston Martin emerging from the dark old days of global recession–the DB9 has proven itself to be a worthy successor. It's a car that has made Aston Martin a true 21st century supercar creator.

29

DB9 V12

Punishing The Prototypes

53 DB9 prototypes were made and put through their paces to ensure that the cars could cut it in extreme climates–from the gruelling conditions of Death Valley and the Arctic Circle through to its mechanics being stretched on the Nürburgring in Germany.

Delight In The Details

The DB9's cockpit has a wealth of quality touches–the glass starter button in the center console shimmers red when the ignition is switched on, and once the engine is turned on the button lights up blue.

VH–Very Handy

From the 'old school' DB7 to the innovative, cutting edge DB9 and beyond–just how did Aston Martin afford it? By creating the über-flexible VH (Vertical and Horizontal) platform–this unique chassis lets Aston change the length of its wheelbase so it can be used on different models (i.e. the larger DB9 or the shorter V8 Vantage).

Personalised For Perfection

Customers have a host of options to choose from when ordering their DB9–there are 29 colors available but Aston Martin will let you choose any you want at an extra cost. As well as a multitude of different leather options, four different woods are also available for the Aston's interior–mahogany, walnut, bamboo and piano black.

Taking A Different Tach

The rev counter featured in the DB9 actually runs anti-clockwise which echoes early Aston Martins such as the Atom and DB2. You won't find a red line on the tachometer either–instead a red light appears once the maximum revs are hit. The reason is another sign of how Aston Martin has moved the game on–electronics detect when that red light should come on depending on ambient temperature, the engine's mileage and how long ago the engine was turned on.

Swan Song

The DB9's doors don't open like the average coupe's–they actually pull upwards at a 12° angle to help the driver gain easier access to the cabin.

Aston Martin DB9: The Specifications

Engine	Fuel injected 48-valve V12	0–100mph	4.9secs (manual) 5.1secs (auto)	Suspension Front	Double wishbones with monutube dampers, coil springs & anti-roll bar	Height	1270mm/50in
Valvetrain	DOHC 4 valves / cyl					Wheels Front	8.5 x19in
Displacement	5935cc	Maximum Speed	186mph			Wheel Rear	9.5 x 19in
Maximum Power	450bhp at 6,000rpm	Steering	Rack and pinion with Servotronic speed-sensitive power-assist	Suspension Rear	Double wishbones with monutube dampers, coil springs & anti-roll bar	Price	£103,000/US$155,000
Maximum Torque	420lb ft at 5,000rpm						
Transmission	Six-speed manual or six-speed auto	Brakes Front	Ventilated & grooved with six callipers/355mm/14in	Kerb Weight	1710kg/3770lbs (manual) 1800kg/3968lbs (auto)		
0–62mph	4.7secs (manual) 4.9secs (auto)	Brakes Rear	Ventilated & grooved with four callipers/330mm/13in	Length	4710mm/185in		
				Width	1875mm/74in		

Aston Martin DBR9

Aston Martin has wanted to return to the international motor racing scene for decades and this is how they are doing it—with the DBR9. Based on the DB9 and featuring the same aluminum chassis, the race car has had some major modifications to make sure it's up to the job of winning major competitions—like they did at Le Mans back in 1959.

The DBR9's engine produces 600bhp compared to the DB9's 450bhp while the suspension set-up boasts up-rated components plus a revised geometry. The car now features carbon brakes and a six-speed sequential gearbox mounted on the rear axle. The DBR9's aerodynamics have been optimised to produce the best possible performance on the track and the panels of the racer are also handmade from carbon fiber composite to ensure the car meets competition weight regulations—it now weighs in at feather-weight 1,100kg/2425lbs compared to the DB9's 1710kg/3770lbs.

Aston Martin Racing is making 12 cars to compete in races across North America, Europe and the Far East, and the DBR9 has already experienced major success on its debut at the 53rd Annual 12 Hours of Sebring, Florida in March where Aston's team gleaned itself a GT1 class victory. If you fancy a slice of the action, do bear in mind that 20 of the DBR9s are also being made available to private buyers.

This is what everyone is calling the new 'baby' Aston, but it's destined to make one very big splash when it finally touches down...

It could be argued that the V8 Vantage is the single most important Aston ever to be built. While the Vanquish and DB9 are designed to be sporting GTs that can deliver extreme comfort while offering superb dynamics, the V8 Vantage is meant to be only one thing–a straight-up, no compromises sports car. It's the most affordable Aston to be made available to the masses with a price of £74,500 (US price upon application), which will put it in line with the likes of the Porsche 911.

Aston Martin V8 Vantage

That's virgin territory for Aston Martin, but by all accounts, they are all set to hit the mark right on the bulls-eye. Using their unique aluminum VH platform, as used by the DB9 but shortened with stiffer suspension, the V8 Vantage has a howling 4.3-liter engine providing the firepower. While the V8 Vantage 'only' features a V8, it can match the V12-driven DB9 because it's lighter–giving it a 0–60 time of 4.8secs and a top speed of 175mph; the V8 Vantage owner won't feel inferior in the company of Ferrari or Lamborghini either, never mind its bigger brother.

Unsurprisingly of course, the interior of the two-seater is up to the typical Aston high standards–the alloy fascia with instrument panel features beautifully finished aluminum. But diehard wood fans won't be disappointed–like the DB9, optional mahogany, walnut or bamboo can be included.

As for the build quality, 78 prototypes have been clocking up 1,500,000 miles between them–suffering the searing temperatures of 48°C in Dubai, and enduring –30°C in Sweden. The Nürburgring, Germany, and the Nardo test track, Italy, have been used to develop and hone the V8 Vantage's handling and performance to ensure that the car delivers on its hype while not breaking down after the first quarter of a mile–in fact, one V8 Vantage was challenged with the task of racking up 5,000 miles round the Nürburgring, which it did without breaking its stride.

While it's not strictly a supercar, as is the case with all Astons, there is something about the V8 Vantage that propels it into that category–perhaps it's the perfect styling created by Henrik Fisker–that long nose, the perfect cut lines and its unquestionable presence. It's exotica defined, and put up against its competitors you have to ask yourself–which one is the more desirable? Which one has that 'X factor' which elevates it beyond mere sports car? The answer is staring you in the face...

It's perhaps telling that if this book had been written five years ago, we may have been hard pushed to feature one Aston Martin, let alone three. Perhaps the reborn Aston Martin shows that the amassed talent based in Modena, Italy, has a new direct competitor for making the ultimate exotica that boasts near-unparalleled desirability–and that new region is known as Gaydon, UK. The name will grow on you, we promise.

"The Aston Martin V8 Vantage is exotica defined, and put up against its competitors you have to ask yourself—which one is the more desirable?

Which one has that 'X factor' which elevates it beyond mere sports car?

The answer is staring you in the face…"

Wait-y Issues...

To make sure the V8 Vantage keeps that important air of exclusivity, production of the car will be capped at 2,500 per year. Expect epic waiting lists–for the driver slapping down his deposit today, you can expect to wait until 2007 before it appears on the driveway.

Designer Departed

The good-looking V8 Vantage was designed by Henrik Fisker (who also designed the DB9). He has since departed Aston Martin and moved to California to set up an automotive design and customization company.

Weight A Minute...

The front-engined V8 Vantage has the spot-on weight distribution and offers the ideal set-up for any self-respecting sports car. The Aston's dry-sump lubrication system means that the engine can be placed lower in the body, meaning a lower center of gravity. The result–better balance and stability.

Aston Martin V8 Vantage: The Specifications

Engine	All alloy quad overhead camshaft 32 valve V8	Maximum speed	175mph	Suspension front	Independent double aluminum wishbones with coil over aluminum monutube dampers & anti-roll bar	Length	4383mm/173in
Valvetrain	DOHC 4 valves / cyl	Steering	Rack and pinion with power assist			Width	1866mm/73in
Displacement	4280cc	Brakes front	Ventilated & grooved steel discs with four- piston monobloc callipers/ 355mm/14in, ABS			Height	1255mm/49in
Maximum power	380bhp at 7,000rpm			Suspension rear	Independent double aluminum wishbones with coil over aluminum monutube dampers & anti-roll bar	Wheels front	8.5 x 18in
Maximum torque	302Ib ft at 5,000rpm					Wheel rear	9.5 x 18in
Transmission	Six-speed manual	Brakes rear	Ventilated & grooved steel discs with four- piston monobloc callipers/ 330mm/13in, ABS			Price	£74,500/ US price upon applicaton
0–60mph	4.8secs			Kerb weight	1570kg/3461lbs		

When Bugatti crashed and burned in the 1990s, a small group of ex-employees decided to take their destiny into their own hands and produce a supercar...

The Edonis is unusual. Not just in the way it looks with its bizarre lines and curves; it's different because B Engineering, the company behind this supercar, isn't interested in becoming a major player that produces exotic machinery. After all, the Edonis is their first and last car. All B Engineering ever wanted the supercar to be was a showcase for cutting edge technology that represented the excellence of both the company and the region where it is built–Modena, Italy, home of the supercar.

B Engineering Edonis

The number of staff may be small but many have worked for some of the greatest supercar makers of all time–Ferrari, Lamborghini and Maserati, to name but a few. In fact, the owner of the company, Jean-Marc Borel, used to be the vice chairman of Bugatti. With such an esteemed collection of experts and engineers under one roof, it's hardly surprising that the Edonis is such a special machine.

B Engineering's links with Bugatti form the core of the Edonis–when Bugatti declared bankruptcy in 1995, 21 leftover carbon fiber tubs from the Bugatti EB110 were acquired by B Engineering to create the Edonis. At the heart of the car's hand-built aluminum body is an extreme engine, an evolution of the EB110's–a 3.7-liter V12 with twin turbochargers, plus a six-speed manual gearbox.

With such power under your right foot, it's hardly surprising that the Edonis is blisteringly quick. How the supercar handles such horse power is also a revelation; with project director, Nicola Materazzi, who is famous for the classic handling of the Ferrari, it's perhaps predictable that the Edonis should become renowned for its precision steering and abundant feel.

Equally important to the car's handling are the tyres that were designed by Michelin. Called the PAX system, the Edonis-specific tyres have shorter than normal sidewalls to aid the super-car's handling.

B Engineering set out to showcase just why the Italians are still regarded as the masters of the supercar–and in the eyes of the supercar aficionados, the Edonis has done just that. While B Engineering won't become an everyday name (or the Edonis the star of teenage males' bedroom walls all over the world), the company has added yet another layer of prestige to Modena, the home of the supercar.

*"The Edonis is B
Engineering's first and
last car. All the company
ever wanted the car to
be was a showcase for
cutting edge technology"*

Record Breaker

A 720bhp version of the Edonis managed to break the circuit record of the Nardo race circuit in Italy by lapping at 223mph.

Named And Famed

The word Edonis is actually the Greek word for pleasure. And only a select few will be privileged enough to experience the car–just 21 will be made. B Engineering decided to make 21 because the Edonis is the first car of the 21st century.

Keeping It In The Family

B Engineering has stayed true to its vision of creating a supercar that uses all the incredible resources of the Modena area–local body builders, casters, upholsterers, pattern makers and others were called in to produce the Edonis.

Perfect Supercar CV

The Edonis's project director, Nicola Materazzi, has a resumé that screams supercar pioneer–he was the main contractor for the likes of Bugatti, and then from 1980, he worked for Ferrari on projects such as the GTO Evoluzione and F40. He was also top dog at Ferrari's F1 research and design division.

B Engineering Edonis (720bhp version): The Specifications

Engine	Twin turbocharged V12	0–100mph	8.2secs	Suspension Front	Double wishbones with coil springs, gas dampers & anti-roll bar	Width	1998mm/79in
Valvetrain	DOHC, 5 valves / cyl	Maximum Speed	223mph			Height	1120mm/44in
Displacement	3760cc	Steering	Rack & pinion with power assist	Suspension Rear	Double wishbones with coil springs, gas dampers & anti-roll bar	Price	£450,000 US price not available
Maximum Power	720bhp at 8,000rpm						
Maximum Torque	590lb ft at 5,250rpm	Brakes Front	Cross-drilled & ventilated discs, ABS/355mm/14in				
Transmission	Six-speed manual			Kerb Weight	1500kg/3307lbs		
0–60mph	4secs	Brakes Rear	Cross-drilled & ventilated discs, ABS/335mm/13in	Length	4350mm/171in		

Is it beauty or the beast? It doesn't really matter, the Enzo defines what the supercar moniker is all about...

Explosive, aggressive, uncompromising–these are just some of the words that roar into your mind when you first see the Ferrari Enzo. Where do you start with such bold statement in supercar design? On its release in 2002, it was perhaps intended as a boast; a flipping of the finger at all the other supercar manufacturers that had been snapping at the heels of Ferrari since the marque began making cars back in 1947.

But being a Ferrari, the Enzo is not all show–it also goes like a beast. With 660bhp produced by an ultra lightweight aluminum 6-liter V12 engine, the Enzo can devour many of its modern day competitors with a 0–60 time of 3.5secs. It almost has enough torque to stop the Earth rotating if you should happen to floor the gas while heading in an easterly direction.

Ferrari Enzo

Named after the company's founder Enzo Ferrari, who died in 1988, the Enzo is the marque's fastest ever road-going car with a top speed of over 217mph, and the looks penned by Pininfarina are pure Formula One drama. There are no luscious curves that one normally associates with a exotic supercar; the Enzo makes its intent clear; that F1 nose, the angular body and those venturis shout to even the most casual of observers that this car is the closest a driver will ever get to feeling like Michael Schumacher.

Ferrari have made sure that the Enzo makes the most of its gigantic power by using its hi-tech ASR traction control system and an F1-style six-speed paddle shift that can snap through the gears in milliseconds. The Enzo's handling is legendary as well–its chassis is constructed from carbon fiber and Kevlar honeycomb, which provides the Enzo with its extreme rigidity and strength; while that F1 nose, with its three air intakes, helps to keep the car glued to the road as it increases in speed, while keeping the V12 cool. Stopping capability is vital for such explosive thrust–and the carbon ceramic brakes with ABS are more than a match for such a punishing job.

Open the Enzo's scissor doors and there's easy access to the carbon fiber and leather cabin. The steering wheel is a F1 fan's idea of paradise with a multitude of F1-style buttons mounted on it for controlling everything from race settings to turning off the ASR (if the driver is feeling brave enough). And for that extra Grand Prix touch, there are LEDs running along the top of the wheel, which act as a rev counter.

The Ferrari Enzo is currently regarded as the most technologically advanced supercar available. There's no question that the Enzo is an evolutionary step towards bringing road and track cars closer together. Perhaps the only concern is how Ferrari will top this.

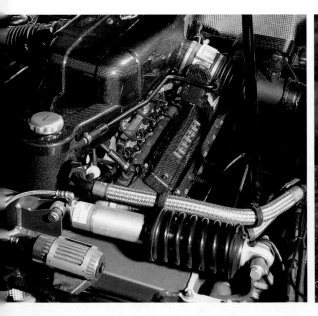

"The Enzo is Ferrari's fastest ever road-going car with a top speed of over 217mph"

51

Going, Going, Gone

Like any respectable supercar, limiting the numbers that can be bought is paramount. Initially, only 349 Enzos were made to order, and Ferrari sold every single one of them before they'd even shown a single picture or spec list of the car. The final figure for the number of Enzos assembled is 400–one more than planned, with the extra car being auctioned off to raise money for the 2004 Asian tsunami appeal.

F1 Champ Elevates Enzo

Formula One champion Michael Schumacher had a firm hand in developing the Enzo. He drove several prototypes of the supercar and gave his thoughts on all aspects of the Enzo, from its performance to the driving position. In fact, thanks to Schumacher, there are 16 different pedal settings available to choose from.

Sky's The Limit

It would appear that the Enzo's value doesn't depreciate–hardly surprising considering the number Ferrari has actually ended up building. But if you want proof–in 2004, the Enzo became eBay Motors' most expensive car ever sold when a Swiss man (bidding from Brazil) made a winning bid of £544,000/US$1,038,227–a brand new Enzo is worth £450,000/US$670,000.

Pulling Power

A survey by the RAC Foundation, based in Britain, discovered that 86 percent of British men would rather spend the weekend with a Ferrari Enzo than hang out with former *Baywatch* star Pamela Anderson. Well, at least the Enzo features more natural materials!

Ferrari Enzo: The Specifications

Engine	Aluminum V12	0–60mph	3.5secs	Brakes Rear	Ventilated carbon-ceramic discs with 4-pot callipers, ABS/380mm/15in	Kerb Weight	1365kg/3009lbs
Valvetrain	DOHC, 4 valves /cyl with Continuously Variable Timing	0–100mph	6.5secs			Length	4702mm/185in
		Maximum Speed	217mph +			Width	2035mm/80in
Displacement	5988cc	Steering	Rack & Pinion with power assist	Suspension Front	Double wishbones with pushrod links, coil springs, gas dampers & anti-roll bar	Height	1147mm/45in
Maximum Power	660bhp at 7,800rpm					Wheels Front	9 x 19in
Maximum Torque	485lb ft at 5,500rpm	Brakes Front	Ventilated carbon-ceramic discs with 6-pot callipers, ABS/380mm/15mm	Suspension Rear	Double wishbones with pushrod links, coil springs, gas dampers & anti-rollbar	Wheel Rear	12 x 19in
Transmission	Six-speed sequential gearbox					Price	£450,000/US$670,000

The F430 had a tough act to follow–Ferrari's illustrious reputation for creating exceptional sports coupés is unrivalled. Think 355 and 360 and mental images of what a sports car should look like pop into your mind immediately. But Ferrari have topped both of these–after all, just in visual terms, it's almost impossible to tear your eyes away from these pictures, isn't it? Some pundits may have complained about the Enzo's angular lines but even they must surely be happy with the F430. Designed by Pininfarina, the 360 Modena replacement is a masterclass in mixing the sensual with the angular, and blending such seemingly diametric elements into a alluring body shape; the back is very Enzo while the front is all scoops and curves.

The Lamborghini Gallardo, the Ford GT and the Aston Martin V8 Vantage... yes, Ferrari may have been facing increased competition over the past couple of years but trust them to come out fighting...

Ferrari F430

The successor to the acclaimed 360, the F430 is constructed entirely from aluminum and features a brand new 4.3-liter V8 engine that boasts far more torque than its forebearer and produces 483bhp–the car has a 0–62 time of 4secs and a top speed of 195mph. The F430 features a six-speed manual as standard and, as an option, a F1 paddleshift that can now move through those gears quicker than the previous incarnation found in the 360.

The F430 also has some new Formula One-sourced tricks up its sleeve for the driver to indulge in. The most obvious is mounted on the steering wheel–the 'manettino'–which is a switch that can be flicked between various different modes–Ice, Wet, Sport, Race and CST–and, as any F1 driver will be familiar with, lets you, with a simple flick, automatically alter the F430's settings such as dampers, traction control plus the speed of the F1 gearshifts (if you have opted for one).

It's clever stuff but that's not all–the F430 also features an electronic differential. A smart alternative to four-wheel drive, this e-diff aids torque distribution to the rear wheels, so if over-keen driving sees the back end starting to slide out, the clutches inside the e-diff quickly send torque to the wheel that has the most traction. Thanks to this unique e-diff, the F430 has none of the on-the-limit tail happiness that the 360 Modena was sometimes known for, and it has been acclaimed for its benign handling and the ability to conquer corners with absolute and utter controllable ease. Not surprising really when you take into consideration the fact that Michael Schumacher had a hand in the car's development.

The interior of the F430 is spot-on for such a thoroughbred–it's all plush leather plus carbon fiber or alloy for the center console. The red starter button can be found on the steering wheel along with that 'manettino' dial. Creature comforts include air-conditioning and a stereo–though how you'd ever get sick of hearing that glorious V8 howl from behind you is quite frankly unimaginable.

The F430 is a genuine step up from the 360–Ferrari knows it can't rest on its laurels with the competition encroaching on its space, but as usual, the Italian stallion has stepped up and thrown down the aluminum gauntlet to its 'foe'. We wonder how the likes of Lamborghini will take to such a challenge.

"The F430 is acclaimed for its benign handling and its ability to conquer corners with absolute ease"

Back To The Future

The F430 features a host of styling cues from Ferrari's rich heritage–the air scoops at the rear pay homage to the 250 LM's, and the two elliptical air intakes at the front are inspired by Ferrari's 1961 F1 racing cars. Even the wing mirrors are similar to the Testarossa of the 1980s. Of course, the Enzo heavily influences the rear layout–the only elements that have remained from the 360 to the F430 are the doors, hood and roof. It's just a shame then that there's a three year waiting list for this fabulous Ferrari.

Wind Up

The F430 is undeniably a beautiful car but, as with any serious supercar, the form follows function. The development of the F430 saw Ferrari's engineers spending over 2,000 hours in a wind tunnel making sure that the aerodynamics of the car were honed to perfection.

A Big Downer

The F430 features a 50 percent increase in downforce when compared to its successor, the 360 Modena. That means stability and safety at high speeds is now vastly improved.

Devil In The Details

It's obvious that Ferrari want owners to bespoke the F430 to their hearts content. Not only can customers turn up with a color sample that they want their car painted in but they can also decide on the tiny details, such as the thread color used inside the car and even the spacing of the actual stitching. And of course, like all supercars, the F430 has its very own luggage set that has been tailored specifically for the car.

Tops Off

A rag top, the F430 Spyder, has joined the F430. While there are always worries about cutting off the roof of a supercar, leaving it structurally compromised, the Spyder has been getting thumbs up all over the media for still being a thrilling drive. And the soft top is electrically operated and so offers quick and easy access to those summer rays.

Ferrari F430: The Specifications

Engine	Aluminum V8	0-62mph	4secs	Suspension front	Double wishbones with coil springs, electrically adjustable tube shocks & anti-roll bar	Width	1923mm/76in
Valvetrain	DOHC, 4 valves / cyl with variable timing and variable intake tract	Maximum speed	196mph			Height	1214mm/48in
		Steering	Rack & pinion with power assist			Wheels front	7.5 x 19in
Displacement	4308cc	Brakes front	Carbon-ceramic discs (optional) with 6-piston callipers / 380mm/15in, ABS,	Suspension rear	Double wishbones with coil springs, electrically adjustable tube shocks & anti-roll bar	Wheel rear	10 x 19in
Maximum power	483bhp at 8,500rpm					Price	£118,500/US$170,000
Maximum torque	343lb ft at 5,250rpm	EBD					
Transmission	Six-speed manual (optional F1 paddleshift available)	Brakes rear	Carbon-ceramic discs (optional), 4-piston callipers/ 350mm/14in, ABS, EBD	Kerb weight	1450kg/3197lbs		
				Length	4512mm/178in		

The Ferrari-beating Le Mans racing legend is reborn and the motoring world falls in love all over again...

It must have been tough for Ferrari when they upset Henry Ford II. After all, the great man was all set to buy the Italian stallion in the early 1960s but alas, the premium sports car marque had a change of heart–and walked away. Bad idea. Ford's reaction to the pullout was the desire to humiliate Ferrari at Le Mans with the creation of the Ford GT40. Built for revenge, Ford managed to thrash Ferrari at its own game by winning the Le Mans 24-hour race four times in a row–from 1966 to 1969.

Ford GT

After such a public dressing down of the world's top supercar, the GT40's legacy was talked about for decades to come. But fast forward to the Detroit Auto Show, USA, in 2002–where the concept of its successor is unveiled– and everyone starts talking again. The world does a double take, pinches itself to make sure that it isn't dreaming and then scrabbles for its chequebook–you see, there's presence and then there's *presence*.

While some woolly-minded critics whined that Ford was merely doing a retro retake on the GT40 and not coming up with any new and fresh ideas for their flagship cars, the rest of us quite frankly couldn't have cared less–the original

GT40 was a beautiful car; but the Ford GT is quite simply stunning.

Sitting close to the ground on its low profile tyres, the GT epitomizes how a proper sports car should look and, with a Ford-claimed 500bhp nestled behind the driver, how it should go as well. With a 0–60 time of 3.7secs and a top speed of 200mph, this is no lukewarm or cynical attempt to cash-in on Ford's heritage by pilfering their classics to make a quick buck–this is a thoroughly updated take on the legendary supercar.

The GT may look dimensionally like the original at first glance but the car is actually 84mm/3.3in taller than its forbearer, and it's wider. And underneath that fine looking exterior is a thoroughly modern all-aluminum spaceframe. Providing the fireworks is a supercharged 5.4-liter V8 mid-engine lump with enough torque to rip tarmac from the road. Or at the very least, rip the rubber off those 19in tyres on the back. After all, the Ford features no traction control or fancy stability systems; driver and passenger air bags and anti-lock brakes are the only concessions to modern 'safe' motoring.

But this really shouldn't be a problem for the driver who treats the GT with the respect it deserves–because the car is renowned for being an absolute cinch to drive through rush hour as well as at full speed. Unlike some of its more 'highly strung' supercar competitors, this car also enjoys being on the limit, and with the GT's chassis, spot-on steering and entertaining handling, has the driving experience to match those damn fine looks too.

Ultimately, what the Ford GT has shown the world is that the blue oval is not just about mass-produced people carriers, city and rep cars –it can also mix it up with the very best in the sports car business and still come out on top.

"*The original GT40 was a beautiful car;
but the Ford GT is quite simply stunning*"

As Good As Old

Like the exterior, the GT's cockpit is a modern take on the old GT40 featuring toggle switches, seats with ventilated seat backs and squabs, and a speedo located above the transmission tunnel.

Fast Forward

To make sure that the GT was ready for their centennial celebrations in 2003, Ford managed to turn the concept car into a production model in a record-breaking 16 months.

Last In Line

Of the 5,000 GTs made, Ford allowed only 85 cars to be shipped over to Europe. The poor old UK had only 24 allocated–so you can only begin to imagine the scrambling of potential purchasers as they tried to get on the fabled shortlist.

The Past Made New

The GT is actually part of Ford's Living Legends range–cars from yester-year given a fresh reworking. Other cars in the series include the glorious-looking Ford Mustang and Thunderbird.

Size Matters

The original GT40 was named so because it was 1016mm/40in tall. The GT has crept up in height to accommodate taller drivers and now stands at 1100mm/43.3in. The height difference aside, if you're wondering why Ford didn't simply stick with GT40 as the name, well, it's because they don't actually own the copyright to it.

Inspired Driving

It has been reported that the designers at Ford wanted the car to offer the image of a Ferrari 360 while retaining the sheer usability of a Honda NSX.

Ford GT: The Specifications

Engine	All-aluminum V8, supercharged	0–100mph	8.3secs	Suspension Front	Double wishbone, mono tube aluminum dampers & anti-roll bar
		Maximum Speed	200mph		
Valvetrain	DOHC 4 valves / cyl	Steering	Rack and pinion		
Displacement	5409cc	Brakes Front	Cross-drilled and ventilated with four-piston callipers, ABS/356mm/14in	Suspension Rear	Double wishbone, mono tube aluminum dampers & anti-roll bar
Maximum Power	500bhp at 6,000rpm				
Maximum Torque	500lb ft at 4,500rpm			Kerb Weight	1519kg/3349lbs
Transmission	Six-speed manual	Brakes Rear	Cross-drilled and ventilated with four-piston callipers, ABS/335mm/13in	Length	4643mm/182in
0–60mph	3.7secs			Width	1953mm/77in

Height	1125mm/44in
Wheels Front	9 x 18in
Wheel Rear	11.5 x 19in
Price	£125,000/US$141,000

Ford GT (2003)

Ford GT40 (1966 Le Mans)

A supercar? From Japan? If you think that only the Europeans make supercars, think again. Honda has been producing one of the world's finest for the past 15 years...

Snobbery is always a terrible thing, but it is the only explanation as to why Honda hasn't been on the receiving end of the kudos it deserves since the NSX was introduced to the world 15 years ago. What you are looking at after all is one of the world's easiest-to-drive supercars. The trouble is that it has a Honda badge on the front and back which, for those with more money than sense, is something of a no-no in a world of Porsches and Ferraris.

Honda NSX

And what a shame—because the mid-engined, rear-wheel drive aluminum-bodied NSX is remarkable. Designed with extensive help from the world's greatest Formula One driver, Ayrton Senna, the car was launched in 1990 to critical acclaim. With a normally aspirated and highly tuned V6 engine (i.e. no turbo or other 'trinkets') welded on, it offered a rev-hungry and thrilling driving experience—when you wanted it.

After all, here's a supercar that can be guided round crowded urban streets at low revs without ever giving you the feeling that it wants to rip your arm off in impatience. Start redlining the NSX though and you'll know why it's a super-car—as with all Honda VTECs, using the full range of the engine rewards the driver with a frenzy of power the higher up the rev range they go. This power delivery is coupled with a rewarding chassis that offers huge grip and balance.

Then there's the reliability—while exotic supercars can demand deep pockets for unexpected 'temperamental' breakdowns, the NSX is Japanese—therefore, reliability comes as standard because Honda know how to screw a car together whether it be a 1.4 Civic or a 276bhp supercar.

The current NSX was introduced in 2002 and has seen the original's pop-up headlamps replaced by fixed headlamps. The current car also has two engines to choose from—the 3.2-liter V6 with a six-speed manual producing 276bhp, and the 3-liter V6 F-Matic version that produces 256bhp.

For the hardcore driver though, the Honda NSX-R is available but only to those willing to import it directly from Japan—a variant that while producing the same 276bhp as the standard car has been completely stripped down. Out has gone the stereo, sound insulation and power locks, to be replaced by race-track stiff suspension, Recaro bucket seats and a smaller battery to name but a few of the changes.

For the supercar driver who wants to experience a (relatively) cheap, comfortable and reliable supercar, the Honda NSX still remains after all this time, the perfect solution. Snobs not welcome.

"The NSX–designed with extensive help from the world's greatest Formula One driver, Ayrton Senna"

David Versus Goliath

It's worth bearing in mind that the NSX was the first time a Japanese car manufacturer had dared to take on the likes of Ferrari–and many would argue that they succeeded.

Senna Sense

While Ayrton Senna was over in Japan in 1989, he was asked to drive a prototype of the original NSX to glean his expert thoughts. According to Honda, he told their engineers: "I'm not sure I can really give you appropriate advice on a mass-production car, but I feel it's a little fragile". Because of that input, the Honda team ended up increasing the car's rigidity by 50 percent.

Going Topless

The NSX is available with a targa top roof as well–the NSX-T–but critics do say that this affects the car's rigidity and that purists should stick to the coupé version. After all, what would Ayrton Senna say?

World First

The NSX was the first production car in the world to feature all-aluminum construction for the chassis, suspension components and chassis, and it is still the only true mid-engine two-seater supercar to come out of the Land of the Rising Sun.

Splitting Hairs

A debate has raged for many years about whether the NSX is a true 'supercar'–detractors believe that it is not powerful enough to warrant the label, while supporters vehemently argue that because of its handling and styling, it most certainly is.

Fighting Talk

The NSX's sleek looks have their origins in the air, not on the road. The original sketches drawn up for the Japanese supercar were actually based on an F16 fighter jet.

Hand-Assembled Heaven

To reflect its special position within Honda, the NSX is hand-assembled in Japan. To make sure the engineers are good enough to put together the supercar, they have to go through a rigorous testing process before being allowed to work on the NSX.

Honda NSX Coupe 3.2 V6 / Acura NSX: The Specifications

Engine	24-valve V6	0–100mph	4.9secs (manual) 5.1secs (auto)	Suspension Front	Double wishbones with monutube dampers, coil springs & anti-roll bar	Height	1160mm/46in
Valvetrain	DOHC VTEC 4 valves / cyl					Wheels Front	7 x 17in
Displacement	3179cc	Maximum Speed	168mph			Wheel Rear	9 x 17in
Maximum Power	276bhp at 7,300rpm	Steering	Rack and pinion with Servotronic speed-sensitive power-assist	Suspension Rear	Double wishbones with monutube dampers, coil springs & anti-roll bar	Price	£59,995/US$90,000
Maximum Torque	220lb ft at 5,300rpm						
Transmission	Six-speed manual or six-speed Auto	Brakes Front	Ventilated & grooved with six callipers/355mm/14in	Kerb Weight	1710kg/3770lbs (manual) 1800kg/3968lbs (auto)		
0–60mph	5.7secs (manual) 4.9secs (auto)	Brakes Rear	Ventilated & grooved with 4 callipers/330mm/13in	Length	4430mm/174in		
				Width	1810mm/71in		

Ferociously fast, perfectly composed and luxurious... ladies and gentlemen, meet Sweden's McLaren F1 slayer with the world's most unpronounceable name...

There's one prerequisite for a supercar—it has to go like hell; and like Hades goes the Koenigsegg. Made in Sweden, the Koenigsegg CC, the dark horse of the supercar world, first broke cover in 2000 and blew the socks and anoraks off the motoring world.

The car is the brainchild of Christian von Koenigsegg who set up the supercar project back in 1993 with a small, dedicated group of enthusiasts. From such humble beginnings emerged the record-breaking monster that you're looking at now. With its latest incarnations, the CC8S and the CCR, that power is now the stuff of legend—the top of the range CCR is officially the fastest production car in the world and can propel you to McLaren F1-vanquishing speeds of beyond 242mph.

Koenigsegg CC

But making a record-breaking car means precious little if the car can't handle such colossal power—thankfully though, Koenigsegg has done its homework here as well. The chassis, made from carbon fiber composite, is renowned for its communicative feedback whether the car's hurtling along at 200mph plus, or being threaded through pot-holed city streets. Then add in the factor that this car is unflappable and perfectly composed on the road—it manages to mix suppleness with practically zero body roll. The end result is a driving experience that never makes the driver feel left out of the loop with what is going on underneath.

While the 'base' model—the CC8S—offers 655bhp, its big brother, the CCR launched in 2004, has a staggering 806bhp on tap and can make the dash from 0–62 in only 3.2secs. This 'extreme' version of the Koenigsegg is achieved by boosting the 'standard' 4.7-liter V8 engine with a bi-compressor centrifugal supercharging system.

You would expect with such explosive power in a hardcore form that you'd find the interior somewhat lacking—that the Koenigsegg options would be limited to a cassette player at best or a floor carpet at worst. Not so with this Swedish supercar—as well as a full leather interior and CD player, the driver can indulge in a wide range of luxuries such as GPS navigation, a rear-view camera, a telephone system and even bespoke suitcases (where you'd put those is another issue altogether). And for those drivers who like the feel of the wind through their hair, open-air thrills are also available because the car comes with a removable roof panel that can be stored under the front hood.

The Koenigsegg offers that rare blend of incredible but utterly exploitable power, and genuine luxury to make the drive of your life the most comfortable possible. Yes, the price tag of £407,000 plus (US price to be confirmed) is a huge amount of cash—but the Koenigsegg is worth every penny. A truly remarkable supercar and virtually unbeatable; never has the phrase 'from zero to hero' been quite so true.

"A truly remarkable supercar and virtually unbeatable; never has the phrase 'from zero to hero' been quite so true"

Full House

The Koenigsegg headquarters are housed in a large fighter jet facility and there are 30 full-time staff. At the moment, seven vehicles can be assembled simultaneously and one car–bearing in mind there are 300-plus carbon fiber parts per car–takes 1,000 hours to assemble.

Door To Door

The carbon fiber doors of the CC open by swinging upwards and resting at a 90° angle. Thanks to gas struts, this operation can be done with a gentle push and also means that the car is easily accessible even in confined spaces.

Record Breaker

In the 2004 edition of the *Guinness Book Of Records*, the Koenigsegg CC8S is listed as the most powerful production car on the face of the planet. This has now been smashed by the 806bhp CCR, which currently holds the world record for the planet's most powerful streetcar.

Have Car, Wheel Travel

The five-spoke magnesium alloy rims featured on the CCR have been specifically designed for Koenigsegg, and the tyres are guaranteed to withstand the strains and stresses of travelling at over 240mph.

Not Too Hot To Handle?

The engineers at Koenigsegg have implemented KACS (Koenigsegg Advanced Control System) as standard on the CCR–this allows the driver to adjust the car's suspension, aerodynamics, road holding and braking components for their preferred set-up.

Koenigsegg CCR: The Specifications

Engine	V8 cast aluminum, supercharged	0–1/4 miles	9secs	Suspension Front	Double wishbones, adjustable VPS custom racing shock absorbers, pushrod operated & anti-roll bar	Kerb Weight	1230kg/2711lb
Valvetrain	DOHC 4 valves / cyl	Maximum Speed	242mph +			Length	4190mm/164in
Displacement	4700cc	Steering	Rack and pinion with power assist			Width	1990mm/78in
Maximum Power	806bhp at 6,900rpm	Brakes Front	Ventilated with six-piston light alloy callipers, ABS/362mm/14in	Suspension Rear	Double wishbones, adjustable VPS custom racing shock absorbers, pushrod operated & anti-roll bar	Height	1070mm/42in
Maximum Torque	678lb ft at 5,700rpm					Wheels Front	9.5 x 19in
Transmission	Six-speed manual	Brakes Rear	Ventilated with six-piston callipers/362mm/14in			Wheel Rear	12.5 x 20in
0–62mph	3.2secs					Price	£407,000/ US price based on customer specification

German build quality partnered with Italian passion... it's an intriguing concept but one that has paid off for the raging bull...

There were some bated breaths in the car community when Audi bought out Lamborghini in 1998– yes, the idea of a car manufacturer known for making bullet-proof pluto barges was a welcome one; perhaps they could temper the sometimes unforgiving nature of Lamborghini's previous cars such as the classic Diablo. But could such a company evolve the iconic supercar marque but keep what makes any Lamborghini so special–the rawness, and the sheer scariness. Or could we end up with a supercar that lacked a certain something? In other words, would the bull be tamed?

Lamborghini Murcielago

All was revealed in 2001 when the result of Lamborghini's and Audi's mating rolled out in front of the public eye. But they need not have worried themselves.

The Murcielago is, yes, more refined and better built but don't start worrying that the Lamborghini has been sanitized. While Audi has ensured that the car has improved safety features and is better built than its predecessors, the Murcielago still has more than enough go to put a cold sweat on the foreheads of even the most experienced driver when taking the car to the limit.

The engine alone will see to that–with 580bhp, the aluminum 6.2-liter V12 is blisteringly quick, and with its four-wheel drive with a central vicious coupler plus traction control, the steel and carbon fiber-built Lamborghini's huge power can be placed down on the road with more ease than its predecessors. The Murcielago also represents a first for the Lamborghini with the inclusion of a six-speed manual gearbox. The car's rear spoiler adjusts depending on the

speed, and those fabulous air intakes mounted on the car's rear shoulders open and close to cool the mammoth engine. And for the show-offs, there's also a dash-mounted button to activate that 'Variable Air-flow Cooling System'.

Lamborghini purists may be slightly disappointed with the car's exterior–but while the aggressive, melodramatic styling of previous Lamborghinis looked like testosterone wrought in metal, the more subtle Murcielago still demands your attention with its clean, simple and muscular lines–it's a thoroughly modern reimagining of the Lamborghini spirit penned by Belgian designer Luc Donckerwolcke.

All this handling and visual drama is backed-up by Audi's obsession with build. The Murcielago was put through a series of punishing tests to make sure that its reliability was up to scratch– while the previous Diablo had only five prototypes racing round the Nardo race track and Sant'Agata in Italy, twelve Murcielagos were taken as far a field as the USA to see how they would bear up under such scorching and harsh temperatures.

It's with this new mindset–the passion of Lamborghini and the build quality of Audi– that the company has matured into a true 21st century supercar marque. With the arrival of the even more desirable and critically acclaimed Roadster version of the Murcielago, the bull is all set to bear down on its competition well into the future.

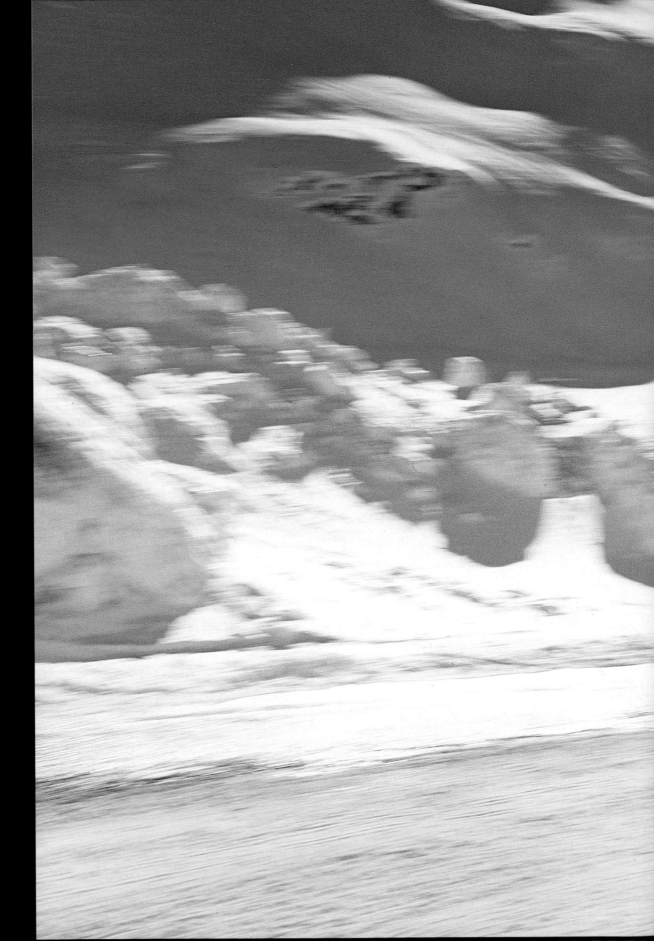

"The Murcielago demands your attention with its clean, simple and muscular lines. It's a thoroughly modern reimagining of the Lamborghini spirit"

What's In A Name?

The Murcielago is named after a bull that fought with the famous matador Rafael Molina 'Lagarttijo' on October 5, 1879. The afore-mentioned bull fought so bravely–and withstood being stabbed 24 times–that the great matador decided to honor the bull and spare its life. The bull was given to a top breeder and the Murcielago lineage continues to this day.

Bullet Proof?

Build quality and reliability were issues that sometimes hovered over the Lamborghinis of old. The now Audi-owned company say that Murcielagos are being driven over 10,000 miles a year by some customers with no problems.

Off With Its Head

Unlike the Diablo Roadster, which horrified the critics on its release, the Murcielago Roadster has taken their breaths away–not only incredible to look at but also a true zero-compromise supercar as well.

All-Wheel Thrills

Lamborghini wanted all the Murcielago's power put firmly down on the road so the driver could enjoy it, and not simply destroy the car's tyres. Subsequently, any excess torque on the rear axle is moved to the front axle to aid the Murcielago get the best traction.

Lamborghini Murcielago: The Specifications

Engine	Aluminum alloy V12	Transmission	Six-speed manual / Optional E-Gear	Brakes Rear	Vented Discs with 4-pot callipers, ABS/335mm	Length	4580mm/180in
Valvetrain	DOHC, 4 valves / cyl with variable-geometry intake system and variable valve timing			Suspension Front	Double wishbones with coil springs, gas dampers & anti-roll bar	Width	2045mm/80in
		0–60mph	3.8secs			Height	1135mm/45in
		0–125mph	8.6secs			Wheels Front	8.5 x 18in
		Maximum Speed	205mph			Wheel Rear	13 x 18in
Displacement	6192cc	Steering	Rack & Pinion with power assist	Suspension Rear	Double wishbones with coil springs, gas dampers & anti-roll bar	Price	£162,000/US$228,000
Maximum Power	580bhp at 7,500rpm						
Maximum Torque	479lb ft at 5,400rpm	Brakes Front	Vented discs with 4-pot callipers, ABS/355mm/14in	Kerb Weight	1650kg/3638lbs		

So, you can't stretch to a Murcielago? There's no need to worry because its baby brother is just as convincing...

Lamborghini Gallardo

Taking on Ferrari and Porsche at their own game is not for the faint-hearted but then again Lamborghini isn't known for pulling any punches. With the backing of owner Audi, the Gallardo was designed to go up against the likes of the Ferrari F430 and Porsche 911. In other words, the Gallardo is supposed to be about potent power on tap with the handling to wring the most out of the 500bhp on offer, all for a price that undercuts its big brother the Murcielago, by a third.

There's no doubt that the Gallardo shares its genes with its big brother but the mini supercar looks more muscular and purposeful with its aluminum bodywork. The car maker wanted to ensure that the Gallardo could be used as a genuine everyday proposition–not simply to be taken out for a spin at the weekend. You won't be surprised to read that Lamborghini pulled it off.

That commute has never been quite so much fun–indeed, this car is easy to manage in the chaos of the rush hour but like any Lamborghini, the Gallardo is designed to be pushed, and heavy-

footing the accelerator shows that this bull hasn't lost its horns. That V10 bellows its way up the rev range, easily managed with the six-speed manual or the optional e-Gear sequential gear shifting system that lets the driver flick through the paddles mounted on the steering column.

This power is delivered by a mid-mounted V10 5-liter engine, which produces 493bhp. Neck-snapping acceleration is mandatory with any Lamborghini, and the Gallardo won't disappoint either with a 0-62 time of 4.2secs and a top speed of 192mph. If anything, there's almost too much power on offer–finding a road long (and legal) enough to work your way up the gears is nearly impossible unless you're hurtling down a German autobahn or flexing the car's muscle on a track.

What's so revered about the Gallardo, and so different to the Countachs of yesteryear, is the sheer controllability of the car–with its low center gravity and all-wheel drive featuring Lamborghini's Viscous Traction system distributing the power between the front and rear wheels depending on road conditions, the Gallardo isn't the kind of supercar that will catch you off guard. Even in the wet, that four-wheel drive system means that the Gallardo rarely has a problem finding traction. Couple such huge grip with the feedback pouring out from the steering wheel and the seat, and the Gallardo driver can make startling progress without feeling intimidated by what they are sitting in.

And sitting in the Gallardo offers no nasty surprises either–Audi-build quality seeps out of the cockpit; with its fully adjustable, electrically operated leather seats, there are enough creature comforts, such as air-conditioning and even optional satellite navigation, for the long-distance driver. The only blot on the landscape is actually accessing that cabin, which may disappoint if you are expecting scissor doors that sweep elegantly up into the air. No, these are, dare we say, just hinged conventional doors–it's obvious that Lamborghini wanted to reserve the fancy stuff for the company's flagship, the Murcielago.

What's most striking about the Gallardo is just how successful Lamborghini has been at muscling its way into traditional Ferrari territory without any compromise in Lamborghini's philosophy. The baby Lamborghini is the most sorted car the company has ever released.

"The Gallardo is designed to be pushed, and heavy-footing the accelerator shows that this bull hasn't lost its horns"

Winging It

The Gallardo's rear wing is able to change its angle depending on how quickly the car is moving. Below 50mph, the wing remains flush with the rest of the Gallardo's bodywork but at 80mph, it shifts upwards to create more downforce. After all, with 500bhp, the Gallardo needs all the stability it can get.

Audi Aluminum

To keep the Gallardo light on its toes, and to ensure rigidity, the supercar's chassis and body are made entirely from aluminum. Audi, pioneers in the use of aluminum in car production, have obviously brought their wealth of knowledge to the creation of the Gallardo.

The Lamborghini A8?

Audi didn't just stipulate the Gallardo's build quality, they also lent their air-conditioning system and stereo; you can normally find them residing in the Audi A8. This might be a cost-cutting exercise for Lamborghini but, at the end of the day, both of the Audi elements are of a very high quality, so Gallardo owners needn't be disappointed.

Instant Hit

It's a blessing for any keen driver who's just taken delivery of their new pride and joy–unlike many cars, the Gallardo's engine needs no 'breaking-in' period before unleashing the car's huge potential. To ensure that drivers can start wringing the most out of the V10's huge power, the engine is actually run in at the factory before being mounted in the Gallardo.

Lamborghini Gallardo: The Specifications

Engine	Aluminum V10	Transmission	Six-speed manual (optional E-gear system available)	Brakes rear	Ventilated discs with 8-piston allipers/335mm/14in, ABS	Kerb weight	1530kg/3373lbs

Engine	Aluminum V10	Transmission	Six-speed manual (optional E-gear system available)	Brakes rear	Ventilated discs with 8-piston allipers/335mm/14in, ABS	Kerb weight	1530kg/3373lbs
Valvetrain	DOHC, 4 valves / cyl with variable intake system & continuously variable valve timing	0-62mph	4.2secs			Length	4300mm/169in
		0-100mph	9.0secs	Suspension front	Double wishbones w/anti-roll bar with coil springs, dampers & anti-roll bar	Width	1900mm/75in
		Maximum speed	192mph			Height	1165mm/46in
Displacement	4961cc	Steering	Rack and pinion with power assist			Wheels front	8.5 x 19in
Maximum power	493bhp at 7,800rpm			Suspension rear	Double wishbones w/anti-roll bar with coil springs, dampers & anti-roll bar	Wheel rear	11 x 19in
Maximum torque	376Ib ft at 4,500 rpm	Brakes front	Ventilated discs with 8-piston callipers/365mm/14in, ABS			Price	£115,000/US$166,000

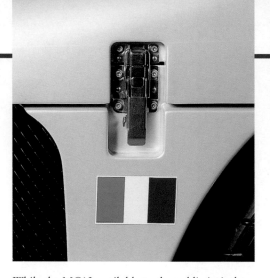

Maserati's heritage is steeped in racing but it's been a long time since the revered marque headed back out onto the track—nearly four decades ago in fact. This road-going MC12 exists in order for a racing version to compete in the FIA Grand Tourer racing class; to qualify, Maserati had to sell 25 road-going versions before it could unleash its GT racetrack car. But how do you go about creating a racing thoroughbred in just a year without breaking the bank?

The car you're looking at is a Ferrari Enzo. Well, it isn't. But it is. Let us explain...

Maserati MC12

Up until recently, Maserati was in partnership with Ferrari and thanks to the Italian stallion, the MC12 has its engineering roots in the legendary Ferrari Enzo. It features the same carbon monocoque, the same V12 engine (albeit detuned), and even the same basic steering wheel and windshield. But before someone mentions 'the emperor's new clothes', the MC12 is aerodynamically superior to the prancing horse. After all, it's 610mm/24in longer and it features extended overhangs at both the back and rear. That means the engineers have been able to optimise how the air flows over (and exits) the MC12's body.

While the MC12 available to the public isn't the actual car that will race round tracks scooping up awards, it's close enough. Surprisingly though, it's been noted just how well behaved the MC12 is–easy gear changes, light steering and a ride that doesn't jar. But hit the accelerator and any illusions of being in a user-friendly runabout vanish quicker than the car hitting 0–60 in 3.8secs. The MC12 boasts an even power delivery so the driver is constantly pinned back in his racing seat as the car thunders its way up to 205mph. The Maserati's stellar progress aided amply by the gear changes made from the paddles situated behind the steering wheel. And needless to say, with a car based on the Enzo, the car handles, offering grip and feedback with perfect body balance.

The interior of the MC12 is an elegant but functional cockpit with lightweight carbon fiber used in abundance, plus striking Milan fashion house-sourced fabric mesh featured liberally on the dashboard. The carbon fiber seats feature full harnesses, and a large rev counter dominates the MC12's dials.

Those hoping to have a back window to glance out of will be disappointed because there isn't one. But you can always whip off the targa top and turn the MC12 into a Spyder–and poke your head up when reverse parking at your local shopping mall.

What's incredible about this supercar is what Masearti managed to achieve in 12 months–it's nothing short of a miracle. Yes, there may be a lot of Enzo genes in the MC12, but thanks to Maserati's exceptional design and engineering, they've created a truly unique supercar, which should help them propel the Trident back into the racing limelight all over again.

"The Maserati MC12 has its engineering roots in the legendary Ferrari Enzo"

Long Time Coming

Maserati, a name synonymous with racing excellence, achieved its last victory way back in 1967 with the Cooper Maserati F1 at the South African Grand Prix. The last time the marque had its very own dedicated Grand Prix team was ten years before that.

Design Guru

While the MC12 was built for functionality rather than creative form, the supercar still has the kind of road presence that shames many of its competitors–it was designed by Frank Stephenson whose last job before joining up with the Ferrari Maserati Group was to design the Mini Cooper.

What's In A Color?

The MC12 is available only in a two-tone white and blue livery. This color scheme is in homage to the Maserati Tipo 60–61 'Birdcages' from the early 1960s.

Keeping Up With The Jones'es

The MC12 is surely the last word in exclusivity–only 50 will ever be made. While the price tag is colossal, you shouldn't be surprised to hear that most have already been sold. Time for interested purchasers to head to eBay then...

Hooked On Air

Like a true Le Mans racer, the MC12 features a large snorkel on its roof and rear grille to shove air down on to the Ferrari Enzo-sourced V12 engine.

Speedy Production

It's claimed that to get the MC12 from the drawing board to the finished car took a year. In fact, every element of creating the car was done at light speed–the alloys took a mere 15 days to go from design to the prototype wheel.

Maserati MC12: The Specifications

Engine	V12	Maximum Speed	205mph	Suspension Front	Double wishbones with push-rod links, steel dampers & coil springs	Height	1205mm/47in
Valvetrain	DOHC, 4 valves / cyl	Steering	Rack and pinion with power assist			Wheels Front	9 x 19in
Displacement	5998cc			Suspension Rear	Double wishbones with push-rod links, steel dampers & coil springs	Wheel Rear	13 x 19in
Maximum Power	622bhp at 7,500rpm	Brakes Front	Cross-drilled & ventilated discs with 6-piston callipers, ABS/380mm/15in			Price	£515,000/ US$770,000 approx.
Maximum Torque	480lb ft at 5,500rpm						
Transmission	Six-speed sequential manual	Brakes Rear	Cross-drilled & ventilated discs with 4-piston callipers, ABS/335mm/13in	Kerb Weight	1335kg/2943lbs		
0–60mph	3.8secs			Length	5143mm/202in		
				Width	2096mm/82in		

With hindsight, it's hard to think how Mercedes could have failed with the SLR. They're not exactly known for producing the four-wheeled equivalent of turkeys in the first place. Then you have Mercedes' racing heritage, which has directly influenced the SLR–its legacy dates back to the 1950s when the company was scooping up racing trophies left, right and dead center with the original SLR Coupe.

And like its forefather, the new SLR pushes out the technological envelope too–a process helped by teaming up with their Formula One partners, McLaren, who are rather well known for producing what is arguably still the greatest supercar of all time–the McLaren F1.

The three-pointed star wanted to make an impact with their first true supercar. Here's how they pulled it off...

Mercedes-Benz McLaren SLR

So with impeccable credentials on both sides, it was perhaps inevitable that the new SLR is a classic, managing to straddle the gap between the ferocious performance of a supercar and the luxuries of a GT. But this is no watered-down compromise–just look over the long dart-like form of the car and its arrow-shaped nose, and

it's not hard to see how the SLR's design elements are clearly inspired by the Formula One Silver Arrows. That full carbon fiber body encases cutting edge mechanics–a hand-assembled super-charged 5.5-liter V8 engine, producing 626bhp (and enough torque to beat its chief rival, the Ferrari Enzo) is mounted towards the front of the chassis. Power delivery is borderline insane–it's been compared to being shot out of a cannon as the car rips its way towards the horizon; the five-speed automatic gearbox effortlessly slicing up through the gears.

Handling is sublime with huge levels of grip coupled with that seemingly endless power delivery–coming out of corners and going hell for leather has never been quite so fast. While the suspension is, of course, firm, the SLR won't send the driver's spine into a jarring spasm–the car effortlessly deals with uneven road surfaces while offering the razor-sharp responses.

The only chink in the SLR's formidable armour is its ceramic brakes–they've been regularly criticized for their complete lack of feel, leaving the driver having to learn how to use the SLR's electronically regulated braking power–not something that you particularly want to do in a supercar that can hit 0–60 in 3.7secs. That said, once mastered, they are highly effective at slowing down in an emergency; a process helped by the SLR's spoiler turning into an airbrake under heavy braking.

Opening the gull wing doors of the SLR reveals a snug interior more in keeping with a luxurious GT rather than a hairy-chested supercar–an optional claret-red leather-swathed interior can be ordered, a color arrangement inspired by the 1950s SLR's interior. Electronically adjustable carbon-frame seats, chronometer-style instruments and the use of carbon fiber and aluminum create an environment that should see drivers happily clocking up hundreds of miles in style.

The SLR is perhaps the best of both worlds–more than enough power and handling for the keen driver to exploit and, more importantly, enjoy while keeping said driver cosseted in GT-style comfort and refinement. It all sounds terribly Mercedes–and that's no bad thing.

"*The new SLR is a classic, managing to straddle the gap between the ferocious performance of a supercar and the luxuries of a GT*"

Smooth Operator

Based on Formula One technology, the SLR's underbody is virtually smooth. That coupled with a six-channel diffuser at the rear means that there is minimal drag and more downforce produced when hitting higher speeds. Even the exhausts have been moved to the side to ensure that aerodynamics aren't affected–those sidepipes also pay tribute to those featured on the 1950s SLR.

Sudden Impact

If an SLR driver should find themselves about to go nose first into an immovable object, they can seek solace in the car's long carbon fiber body and front end crash structure, offering the kind of energy absorption in crashes that has saved many lives on the Formula One circuit.

Acronym Explained

During the SLR's heyday in the 1950s, the SLR stood for Sporty Light Racer.

"How do I start this?"

Like all classic supercars, the SLR has the obligatory starter button. Instead of being mounted in the central console, the glowing red starter button is actually located on the end of the gear lever–simply flip back the cover and push down.

Geared For Action

The five-speed auto gearbox sourced from the Mercedes-owned luxury limo, the Maybach, comes with two automatic settings and three manual ones. The manual settings can be accessed via the gear lever or the steering wheel-mounted buttons.

Mercedes 'First' Supercar

The SLR isn't in fact Mercedes' first supercar. Back in 1991, Mercedes were all set to unleash the C112, a supercar with 500bhp that could break the 200mph barrier. Alas, the company eventually decided that the car simply wasn't right for the Mercedes' image and it was canned.

Mercedes-Benz SLR: The Specifications

Engine	AMG V8	0–125mph	10.7secs	Suspension Front	Double wishbones with coil springs & gas dampers
Valvetrain	SOHC, 3 valves / cyl	Maximum Speed	208mph		
Displacement	5439cc	Steering	Rack & pinion with power assist	Suspension Rear	Double wishbones with coil springs & gas dampers
Maximum Power	626bhp at 6,500rpm	Brakes Front	Fiber reinforced ceramic discs with eight piston callipers, ESP, SBC/ 370mm/14.5in	Kerb Weight	1768kg/3898lbs
Maximum Torque	575lb ft at 3250–5000rpm			Length	4656mm/183in
Transmission	5-Speed Auto with Speedshift System			Width	1908mm/75in
		Brakes Rear	Fiber reinforced ceramic discs with 4 piston callipers, ESP, SBC/360mm/14in	Height	1261mm/50in
0–60mph	3.7secs				

Wheels Front	9 x 18in
Wheel Rear	11.5 x 18in
Price	£313,465/US$455,000

The Mitsubishi should probably be reserved for the final chapter about cars that boast supercar performance for a fraction of the cost; but the models found lurking in the Mitsubishi Lancer Evolution VIII range offer such outrageous performance and spot-on handling, that they make the Evo a genuine (if left-of-center) supercar contender.

The VIII range features the VIII 260 'base' model, which is more than enough for most of us to enjoy on a regular basis. Mitsubishi though is famous for 'tweaking' its cars and has subsequently produced upgraded VIIIs, including the FQ-300 and FQ-340.

While supercars can trace their DNA back to the race track, the Evo range was born out of the mud, gravel and pot holes of rallying...

Mitsubishi Lancer Evolution VIII

The latest edition–the Evo VIII FQ-400–can produce a G-force that would give the sort of Hollywood facelift that an aging actress would kill for. In the 3.5secs it takes to hit 60mph, your skin is pulled back so far that you'll look ten years younger; the trouble is that it could also age you if you're not up to handling the Evo's huge power.

While the FQ-400 may be easy to handle driving round town at low revs, hit the magic power band at 5,000rpm, and the turbo kicks in properly –well, 'kicks off' actually. Once the turbo is churning out its power through the rally-sourced four-wheel drive, you won't be able to believe that it's all coming from a 2-liter turbo-charged engine. Look at the spec list and you'll see that this car produces a whopping 405bhp. Not bad considering what is under the skin–a humble sedan car.

Of course, being a rally car designed for the road, the Evo can do the twisty stuff as well as the 0–100mph assault on your senses–with neutral handling, tidy body control and colossal grip, the Evo can devour corners with unnerving confidence. Many argue though that the FQ-400 is simply too extreme and that FQ-340 version will give you great performance but of the sort that can be used more frequently on the average trip to the supermarket. But perhaps the FQ-400 harks back to the good/gory old days of the supercar when zero fear of losing your driving licence (and spending long stretches in prison) was required to fully exploit the car's talents.

But for all the raw power on offer in the FQ-400, you might be surprised to hear that the makers of Evo have put their money where their mouth is when it comes to warranties. Remember that this is a Japanese car so reliability comes as standard –but this extreme engineering of the Evo has the benefit of being backed-up by a cast-iron three year/36,000 miles warranty–that even includes drivers who've taken to tearing their Evos round tracks on a regular basis.

While Europe may be seen as the home of the supercar with its exotic design and elegant engineering, the Evo is the Japanese equivalent of putting a single finger up to such svelte stallions. There's no pretension, no disillusions of grandeur–this is hardcore.

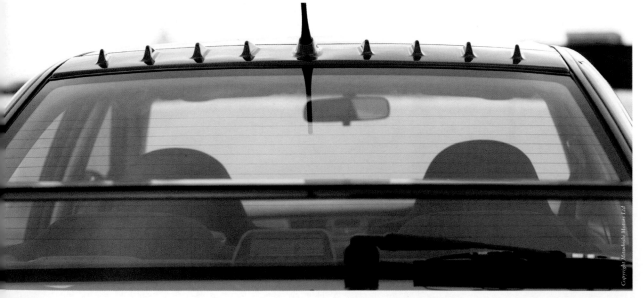

Copyright Mitsubishi Motors Ltd

"Being a rally car designed for the road, the Evo can do the twisty stuff as well as the 0–100mph assault on your senses. With neutral handling, tidy body control and colossal grip, the Evo can devour corners with unnerving confidence"

Frightfully Quick

The MR stands for 'Mitsubishi Racing' but ever wondered what the FQ in the MR FQ-400 stands for? Hmm, tough question—we can confirm that the Q stands for 'quick', but the 'F'? Perhaps it means 'frightfully' or 'freaking', or perhaps something decidedly cruder. We'll leave it to your imagination...

Number Crunching...

The Pagani Zonda cranks out a very respectable 76.12bhp per liter. The Porsche Carrera GT manages 106.75. The FQ-400 claims 202.5bhp per liter. The Japanese certainly know how to get the most from their engines. And knowing Mitsubishi, they will at some point in the very near future top that too. They really can't help themselves, thankfully...

Need For FQ Speed

The FQ-400 is not only the fastest road-going car that Mitsubishi has ever made (for the UK market at least)—it also has the honor of being the fastest accelerating four-door sedan, from a major manufacturer, ever to grace public roads.

Ready To Launch

To keep the FQ-400's immense power welded to the road, instead of coming off at the first corner, Mitsubishi's engineers have made sure that the car remains stable at high speeds with the inclusion of a carbon fiber front lip spoiler, Ralliart aero mirrors and the rather menacing rear vortex generator—the 'shark's teeth' that can be found poking out of the rear of the roof.

So Little, So Much

Just how did Mitsubishi manage to get so much brake horse power out of 2-liter engine? The most important element is the Garrett turbocharger made especially for the FQ-400, and the engine has also been strengthened to withstand the huge forces needed to develop 405bhp.

How To Handle Yourself...

Mitsubishi don't want customers simply roaring off into the distance in their new purchase—they offer free driver-training courses as part of the asking price so that customers know how to exploit the car's potential safely. Driving instructors are on hand to show how to corner the Evo without ending up at the top of a tree...

Copyright Mitsubishi Motors Ltd

Mitsubishi Lancer Evo VIII MR FQ-400: The Specifications

Engine	Inline-4	0-100mph	9.1secs	Suspension front	McPherson strut suspension with inverted shock absorbers, stabilizer bar & aluminum front lower arms	Length	4490mm/177in
Valvetrain	DOHC turbo with intercooler	Maximum speed	175mph			Width	1770mm/70in
		Steering	Rack and pinion with power assist			Height	1450mm/57in
Displacement	1997cc			Suspension rear	McPherson strut suspension with inverted shock absorbers, stabilizer bar & aluminum front lower arms	Wheels Front	8 x 17in
Maximum power	405bhp at 6,400rpm	Brakes front	Alcon 6-pot monobloc brake kit / 343mm/13in			Wheel Rear	8 x 17in
Maximum torque	355lb ft at 5,500rpm	Brakes rear	Ventilated discs with 2-pot aluminum callipers/ 300mm/12in			Price	£46,999 Not available in the US
Transmission	Six-speed manual			Kerb weight	1400kg/3086lbs		
0-60mph	3.5secs						

109

It looks more than modern—in fact, the Zonda looks like it could have been plucked straight from the pages of some sci-fi magazine, so vividly different does it look from its road-going competitors. But the origins of the car actually date back decades—after all, its Argentinean creator Horacio Pagani was only 12 when he first began making models of supercars from wood and moulded clay, and by the age of 20, he had already constructed his first race car for Renault.

Exotic, outlandish, eccentric... the Zonda is the most individual supercar the world has ever seen...

Pagani Zonda

Now firmly ensconced in the 21st century, the lucid teenage dreams of Horacio have managed to create what many argue is the world's finest supercar. First revealed at the Geneva Motor Show, Switzerland, in 1999, the prototype of the Zonda was always going to cause a fuss—with those alien looks, it simply couldn't fail not to.

But its extraordinary beauty isn't merely skin deep. It's worth bearing in mind that Horacio made a name for himself at Lamborghini before then heading off to create his own automobile design and engineering company, Modena Designs, in 1991, which specialized in lightweight composites. Always on the cards though was the Pagani supercar company and with Horacio's specialist knowledge, the Zonda has an impeccable pedigree.

Unsurprisingly then, at the heart of the car is its unique use of composite materials with a carbon fiber chassis and body, ensuring an incredibly lightweight and rigid structure. Add into that a bullet-proof, smooth-revving Mercedes-Benz AMG V12—after all, those Germans know how to build a reliable engine that won't blow up when you're attempting to top 200mph. The original five-speed C12 had 389bhp on tap in 6.9-liter form and has been constantly evolving ever since. The six-speed Zonda C12 S which is shown here has now evolved into the S 7.3—all 555bhp of it boasting a 0–60 time of 3.6secs. Traction control is included, which is mighty handy for nailing all that power to the road in wet conditions

Perhaps the most keenly anticipated Pagani was the 555bhp Roadster—but there was a genuine concern among fans that chopping off the roof of the Zonda would leave its handling horribly compromised. But again, Pagani and his team managed to blow away any concerns by introducing a new carbon fiber central chassis structure, and a roll bar made from carbon and chrome-molybdene to ensure that rigidity remained at the heart of the Zonda Roadster's winning formula.

The most extreme Zonda was introduced in 2005 —the F version. Built alongside the standard Zonda, it features a lighter chassis and better aerodynamics courtesy of a host of changes including a larger front splitter. That monster Mercedes engine is now even more powerful thanks to a new induction system which means you've got a whopping 602bhp under your right foot—the power-hungry driver wanting even more face-stretching acceleration can of course settle for the Clubsport edition that boasts 650bhp.

For all its firepower though, what makes the Zonda supercar truly exceptional is that while it can lap tracks with the best of them, it also boasts the comfort, and just as important, the reliability of a GT car.

The culmination of Horacio Pagani's dream is now a supercar that can hold its own when put up against the established names like Porsche, Lamborghini and Ferrari. And that is one hell of an achievement.

"*The Zonda was always going to cause a fuss. With those alien looks, it simply couldn't fail not to*"

Exclusivity Guaranteed

The Roadster is regarded as the most desirable of the Zonda range, so interested customers are recommended to put their money down quickly–after all, the Roadster's production will be capped at only 40.

What's In A Name?

What's a supercar without a suitably evocative name? The word Zonda actually comes from a warm wind that blows west across the Andes Mountains in South America.

In Good Company

The Zonda's creator Horacio Pagani had expert help from the now-deceased Grand Prix racing legend, Juan Manuel Fangio. He is credited with aiding Horacio with all aspects of the supercar's creation–from its styling to its world-class handling.

Bespoke Heaven

The interior of the Zonda is as unique as its exterior with its mix of aluminum, leather and carbon fiber. Of course, for that special supercar touch, the company also provides owners with bespoke leather luggage and a pair of driving shoes with every car.

Leap Of Faith

Talk about conviction–Horacio Pagani was so sure that the Zonda would be a hit with the public once they'd seen it at the 1999 Geneva Motor Show, that he'd already had the car crash tested and ramped up ready for production. His instincts proved correct–only months after its unveiling, he had enough orders to take up two years' worth of the car's production.

Pagani Zonda S 7.3: The Specifications

Engine	V12	0–100mph	Sub 8secs	Suspension Front	Double wishbones with helical springs, hydraulic dampers & anti-roll bar
Valvetrain	DOHC 4 valves / cyl	Maximum Speed	220mph		
Displacement	7291cc	Steering	Rack and pinion with power assist		
Maximum Power	555bhp at 5,900rpm			Suspension Rear	Double wishbones with helical springs, hydraulic dampers & anti-roll bar
Maximum Torque	553lb ft at 4,050rpm	Brakes Front	Ventilated with four-piston callipers, ABS/355mm/14in		
Transmission	Six-speed manual			Kerb Weight	1350kg/2976lbs
0–60mph	3.6secs	Brakes Rear	Ventilated with four-piston callipers, ABS/355mm/14in	Length	4395mm/173in

Width	2055mm/81in
Height	1151mm/45in
Wheels Front	9 x 18in
Wheel Rear	13 x 18in
Price	£350,000 US$457,000 estimated

Sports car maker Porsche had been out of the supercar game for nearly two decades. Trust them to come storming back onto the scene with a road racer that makes all the right noises...

It's been a long while coming–the last time Porsche unleashed anything resembling a true supercar on to the world stage was with the magnificent 959 back in 1987. Perhaps we would have had to wait even longer if Porsche hadn't abandoned its Le Mans race car project at the end of the 1990s, which subsequently gave birth to this road-going car.

The GT's racing heritage is apparent throughout the car–it's got Formula One-style all-wishbone pushrod suspension, a brand new V10 engine (that was initially bound for Le Mans), and a small ceramic clutch that's mated to a six-speed manual transmission. Thanks to that diminutive clutch, it means the engine can be mounted lower in the car; the end result being better weight distribution and aerodynamics.

Porsche Carrera GT

Unlike the normally rear-engined Porsches, the V10 is mounted in the middle and produces 612bhp. The low weight carbon fiber monocoque chassis coupled with such power means that the GT can do the 0–60 sprint in 3.8secs and 0–100 in a mere 6.9secs. Porsche also decided that any driver's aids should be thrown out of the window at their factory in Leipzig, Germany- only traction and anti-spin control are included so that the all-important GT driving experience is undiluted.

And the driving experience is what has shaken and stirred supercar aficionados–while in a straight line, the likes of the Ferrari Enzo may just have the Porsche licked, on the twisty stuff though, the GT comes into its own offering a benign drive that is all about feel and communication, coupled with huge grip.

City driving needn't be a handful either with the car willing to idle along before you decide to floor the accelerator and be pushed back into the seat with its startling but ultimately progressive grunt–there are no nasty surprises awaiting the keen, experienced driver.

The interior of the GT is your typical masterclass in Porsche efficiency–you can forget over-indulgent supercar flamboyance distracting you from the road–but looking up, you'll find a removable two-piece hard top that stows under the front hood.

No one should be surprised that Porsche have managed to pull off a masterstroke with their supercar entry–the GT shows just what we've all been missing out on while Porsche has been in supercar hibernation. It's just a shame it took them so long to rejoin the party. Welcome back Porsche–we've missed you.

"On the twisty stuff, the GT comes into its own offering a benign drive that is all about feel and communication coupled with huge grip"

Touching Wood

A Porsche with a wood gear knob? It may seem out of place in a car that uses the latest composite materials, but that gear knob is a nod to the 1970–1971 Le Mans champ, the Porsche 917. So, why wood in the 917? Because it was the lightest material of that time–and it stopped the driver from scalding his hand when shifting gears.

Suited And Booted

There is space under the front hood for luggage in the GT but don't expect to be able to pack any kind of suitcase in there–after all, there are three radiators up front. In the meantime, Porsche provides a specially tailored travel bag to fit into the limited space.

Wheely, Wheely Good

To make a supercar, you have to be weight-obsessed–and Porsche is the 'supermodel' of supercars. For example, unlike most supercars that use aluminum alloy for their wheels, Porsche has used lighter forged magnesium. And those wheels need to be as light as possible –after all, they measure 19in at the front and a whopping 20in at the rear.

VIP: Very Important Porsche

As should be the case when collecting a hugely expensive supercar, you can opt for the factory delivery program where you can pick the car up from the factory based in Leipzig, Germany, and head out on to their test track.

Perfect Service

Potential owners could be forgiven for thinking that a supercar will need constant attention every couple of thousands of miles. Porsche claim that the GT requires the engine oil and air filter to be changed only every 12,000 miles; and the oil filter every 24,000 miles; and the spark plugs every four years or 24,000 miles.

Porsche Carrera GT: The Specifications

Engine	Aluminum V10	0–100mph	6.9secs	Brakes Rear	Porsche Ceramic Composite Brake (PCCB). Ventilated and cross-drilled with six-piston callipers, ABS/ 380mm/15in	Kerb Weight	1380kg/3042lbs
Valvetrain	DOHC 4 valves / cyl with VarioCam	Maximum Speed	205mph			Length	4,613mm/182in
		Steering	Rack and pinion with power assist			Width	1,921mm/76in
Displacement	5733cc					Height	1,166mm/46in
Maximum Power	612bhp at 8,000rpm	Brakes Front	Porsche Ceramic Composite Brake (PCCB). Ventilated and cross-drilled with six-piston callipers, ABS/ 380mm/15in	Suspension Front	Double wishbones with inboard springs inc. dampers units	Wheels Front	9.5 x 19in
Maximum Torque	435lb ft at 5,750rpm					Wheel Rear	12.5 x 20in
Transmission	Six-speed manual with two-plate ceramic dry clutch			Suspension Rear	Double wishbones with inboard springs inc. dampers units	Price	£323,000/US$440,000
0–60mph	3.8secs						

It's loud; it's rude; it's not one for small talk, and it doesn't want to be everyone's friend... it's a TVR then...

The seaside town of Blackpool, in the northwest of England, is not your typical setting for a supercar maker, but amongst the tourist attractions and arcade venues (and donkey rides) is one of the true greats–TVR. Never mind the sticks of rock that can be bought from any Blackpool tourist shop–it's the sticks of automotive dynamite created by TVR that grab the attention of any discerning car fan. And the new Sagaris is no different...

TVR Sagaris

Visually, TVR doesn't do subtle, and the Sagaris is like being poked in the eye with an electric cattle prod–it's that shocking; it makes supercars such as the Ferrari F430 look everyday and hum-drum. Even the eccentric Pagani Zonda might have a tough time in the "what the hell is that?" stakes as passers-by gawp at the spectacle that is the Sagaris. Look over the composite GRP bodywork of the TVR and your senses are assaulted from every angle–those dragon-esque headlamps, the mass of hood vents; and on the car's rump, well, have you ever seen a transparent rear spoiler? No, we thought not.

On looks alone then, the Sagaris is on another level–and underneath, there's typical TVR fire-

power on offer for the brave-hearted driver. The Sagaris was intended to be a trackday car born out of the pretty TVR T350 that would also be suitable for road use; and with the finished car now bedazzling drivers, TVR has delivered on that promise.

With its 0-60 time of 3.7secs and 0-100 in 8.1secs, the 400bhp 4-liter engine mounted on the Sagaris's tubular steel chassis is easy to exploit with its five-speed gearbox. But for all its obvious drama, the Sagaris is day-to-day useable. While threading in and out of traffic, the car is not trying to scrabble to get away from you; however, show it the right road, and the Sagaris demonstrates its true TVR roots. Of course it's very quick with huge grip but, unlike previous razor-sharp TVRs, it won't grow impatient with your bad driving and suddenly decide that a ditch is preferable to the road. The Sagaris gives the driver plenty of warning if things are about to go wrong. That said, you're behind the wheel of a TVR–so don't expect it to generously forgive your every mistake.

Inside the Sagaris is equally special–two white dials peer out at the driver from the dashboard while the rest of the cabin is smothered in leather. Everything on view is bespoke–apart from the three-spoke steering wheel. You'll also notice the roll cage, there to 'reassure' anyone that while the car lacks electronic safety devices, you'll be well looked after if the worst does happen.

The Sagaris is one of two TVRs to come out of the Blackpool company since it was taken over in 2004 (see p.128), and judging by this and the Tuscan 2 featured in the next chapter, the marque shows every sign of going from strength to strength under its new leadership. With its unmatched 'butch' charisma, no BS approach and obscene performance, the low volume British TVR range is something to be cherished; God bless the (melodrama) Queen.

"Visually, TVR doesn't do subtle, and the Sagaris is like being poked in the eye with an electric cattle prod. It's that shocking; it makes supercars such as the Ferrari F430 look everyday and hum-drum"

Name Dropping

The marque's lack of pretension is perfectly illustrated by the origins of the company's name—TVR. It's not some acronym for a fancy design philosophy but is actually based on the founder's first name, TreVoR Wilkinson.

A Brief (Recent) History Of TVR

TVR was founded in 1947—but in 2004, the company was sold to a 24-year-old entrepreneur, Nikolai Smolenski, who, at the last count, was worth nearly £55 million/US$105 million. His initial moves to take TVR into the 21st century have been to address the build quality issues that have plagued the handmade TVRs of the past; because customers have been put off by reliability issues, the Russian delayed the release of the Sagaris and the Tuscan 2 to ensure that build quality was improved.

Bound For The USA?

While TVR has amassed a cult following in the USA thanks to games such as PlayStation 2's *Gran Turismo* series and movies like *Swordfish*, the car isn't available to the US public. Only time will tell if the new owner of TVR has plans to unleash the brand in America.

"I'm A TV-R Star"

The Sagaris prototype unveiled to thrilled audiences in 2003 went on to become one of the stars of British reality TV show *The Heist* where ex-criminals were charged with the task of stealing it. They succeeded.

Keeping It Close

The factory in Blackpool, England, makes practically everything you see inside and outside of a TVR, and the company's straight-six engines are the stuff of motoring legend. TVR is obsessed with doing as much of the cars as possible by using local talent and skills.

TVR Sagaris: The Specifications

Engine	All-aluminum TVR Speed Six straight-six	Maximum speed	175mph	Suspension front	Independent double wishbones with coils over gas hydraulic dampers & anti-roll bar	Length	4057mm/160in
Displacement	3996cc	Steering	Rack and pinion with power assist			Width	1850mm/73in
Maximum power	406bhp at 7,000-7,500bhp	Brakes front	Ventilated discs with 4-piston alloy callipers/322mm/13in			Height	1175mm/46in
Maximum torque	349lb ft at 5,000rpm			Suspension rear	Independent double wishbones with coils over gas hydraulic dampers & anti-roll bar	Price	£49,995 US price not available
Transmission	Five-speed manual	Brakes rear	Ventilated discs with single sliding piston calipers/ 298mm/12in				
0-60mph	3.7secs						
0-100mph	8.1secs			Kerb weight	1078kg/2376lbs		

Now in its second generation, the Tuscan has 'grown up' to become a more civilized supercar than the hooligan-like original. But the beast still lurks beneath those strikingly beautiful looks...

The shape of the Tuscan is a classic–it's sensual; it's individual; indeed, psychologists could probably argue for hours about how Freudian the Tuscan is. But all you need to know is that it's an update of the utterly seductive design that was first featured on the original Tuscan–it screams out brute force from every curve.

Featuring TVR's incredible straight-six engine that produces a whopping 350bhp, the Tuscan 2 is blindingly fast–0-60 takes 4.2secs, and the supercar will happily see 175mph and beyond. But TVR's engineers aren't known for sitting back and slapping themselves on the back for a job well done; they've been busy 'tinkering' and have produced the top of the range Tuscan 2 S that features 400bhp on tap and can hit 0–60 in 3.8secs–goodbye Gallardo. All that power is kept on the road at high speed thanks to a splitter under the front grille and a gurney above the trunk lid which ensures downforce over both the front and rear axles.

TVR Tuscan 2

But be under no illusion, the Tuscan 2 S (and the 2 for that matter) isn't a supercar that likes to cosset its drivers–while the Tuscan 2 has been designed to be more 'soft' around the edges than the original, this is still a hugely aggressive car that, compared to its competitors, is as hardcore as they come. The Tuscan 2 will still intimidate the inexperienced driver–it will even have the hugely experienced breaking out a nervous grin when taking the car right to the limit; driving on the limit requires focus and concentration, and there's precious little safety equipment on board if it all starts to go pear-shaped–no traction control, no ABS, no, well, anything–just an integrated roll-cage. The Tuscan is no pussycat but no TVR ever should be.

Climb inside the TVR and the sight of a fully bespoke interior will greet you; all the vital readouts such as speed and revs are digital; the leather upholstery is made by TVR in-house, and the alloy switchgear is tactile and satisfying to use. There is an issue though for anyone familiar with the TVR brand–build quality. Some have said that a TVR is best to use as a weekend car because you sure wouldn't want to rely on it getting you to work day-in, day-out.

The development of the TVR Tuscan 2 and the Sagaris though saw them being put through punishing conditions in Bahrain, South Africa, Saudi Arabia and Russia for the first time to ensure that the car could take high speeds in gruelling environments. Whether all the 'gremlins' have been wiped out remains to be seen though–only time will tell but with its three year/36,000 mile warranty, TVR is backing up its new found commitment to build quality with its bank balance.

So the TVR Tuscan 2 is something special–its looks, coupled with its outrageous performance, mean that this a true old school supercar. It might have softened up but still treat it with the respect it deserves and you are guaranteed to have the drive of your life. Treat it with contempt, and it will bite back. A true British bulldog then.

"Driving a TVR on the limit requires focus and concentration, and there's precious little safety equipment on board if it all starts to go pear-shaped—no traction control, no ABS, no, well, anything—just an integrated roll-cage. The Tuscan's no pussycat but no TVR ever should be"

Doing It Differently

TVR is known for not playing by the rules with any element of its cars. They even have to do their doors differently–don't go looking for a traditional handle by the way; pushing a button underneath the wing mirror makes the window slip down, the door gently springing open. Now how's that for 'bespoke'?

Bark Worse Than Its Bite?

The TVR's straight-six engine sounds incredible–the deep roar that bellows every time you floor the car is a marvel–but the original Tuscan could bite in the handling department. The Tuscan 2 features a revised geometry, improved bump stops plus re-rated springs and dampers so that the car can be manhandled more easily when pushing the Tuscan 2 to its limits. But still, it's advised that the TVR is handled with care.

Practical As Well As Powerful

Many supercars require you to shoe-horn any luggage into them using either bespoke bags... or a crowbar. The Tuscan 2 however can happily take two golf bags, which means the car's actually practical as well as sensational.

Lighten Up

The key to the Tuscan 2's searing performance is the fact that it weighs so little–with a kerb weight of only 1,100kg/2425lbs to cart around, that 4-liter straight-six engine can offer supercar performance without the need for added extras like turbo chargers.

TVR Tuscan 2: The Specifications

Engine	All-aluminum TVR Speed Six straight-six	**Maximum speed**	175mph	**Suspension front**	Independent double wish bones with coils over gas hydraulic dampers & anti-roll bar
Displacement	3605cc	**Steering**	Rack and pinion with power assist		
Maximum power	350bhp at 7,200rpm	**Brakes front**	Ventilated discs with 4-piston alloy callipers/ 304mm/12in	**Suspension rear**	Independent double wish bones with coils over gas hydraulic dampers & anti-roll bar
Maximum torque	290lb ft at 5,500rpm				
Transmission	Five-speed manual	**Brakes rear**	Ventilated discs with single sliding piston calipers/ 282mm/11in		
0-60mph	4.2secs			**Kerb weight**	1100kg/2425lbs
0-100mph	9.5secs				

Length	4235mm/167in
Width	1810mm/71in
Height	1200mm/47in
Wheels Front	8 x 16in
Wheel Rear	8 x 16in
Price	£39,850 US price not available

Future Perfect?

It seems like we've hit perfection with the supercar. So where do you go from here? How do you top what seems insurmountable? Well, judging from the various developments and news (and a fair smattering of rumours too), the best is inevitability still to come. The supercar community's desire to outdo each other and seduce buyers will see the arrival of more potential supercar classics over the next few years.

For example, McLaren is all set to re-enter the scene aproper in 2008 with its supercar codenamed the P8. Featuring a Mercedes-sourced 6.3-liter V8, the P8 should be able to produce above 500bhp and over 440lb ft of torque, all for the estimated price of £150,000/US$200,000.

Then there are the left-of-the-middle entries such as Project 1221's MF1. Details are scant about this emerging supercar but the makers claim it will have unmatched handling and agility plus a large luggage capacity. Yes, you may have heard such hyperbole a dozen times before but the MF1 could actually deliver. After all, it's being engineered by the former technical director of Lamborghini and Bugatti, Mauro Forghieri.

As for the far future, there's that 300mph barrier to break, and it has been predicted that supercars will produce in excess of 2,000bhp, weigh 25 percent less than current crop and could even hit 350mph. Sounds like the ramblings of the mad but there is a supercar that's set to touch down later this year which could potentially leave the outrageous performance of current supercars for dead, and offer an enticing and very real glimpse of what the future of the supercar has in store for us.

It shouldn't really be featured in this book–after all, the Bugatti Veyron has been on the verge of hitting the road for what seems like years. Hounded by delays and slips in production, it's become something of a running joke in the auto industry that it will never actually see the light of day.

Fact or fiction? The latest legend to bear the Bugatti name could finally be with us after a very long development period...

The trouble is that the industry also happens to be head over heels in love with the Veyron, and who can blame them? First of all, the Veyron is the latest creation from a brand that has fans all over the world–Bugatti was created back at the beginning of the 20th century by Ettore Bugatti; its limos and sports cars from the 1920s and 1930s are now the stuff of motoring legend. And so is the company's history.

Copyright Bugatti Automobiles S.A.S.

Bugatti Veyron

Death in the Bugatti family; a failed revival; and a rebirth followed by a humiliating bankruptcy when the world sank into recession in the 1990s–reading Bugatti's history, you could be forgiven for thinking that the company is cursed. Even in the hands of Volkswagen, the development of the latest car to bear the Bugatti name–the Veyron–was at one point halted. But now VW has the car back on track with delivery of the

first Veyron to one lucky (and rich) customer at the end of 2005.

Any supercar fan knows why it's essential that the Veyron does finally touch down–after all, it could potentially rip asunder every supercar that's gone before it. Here are the figures–it's got nearly 1,000bhp on tap; it's got not one, but 4 turbos; it's expected to weigh in at just under 2 tonnes; it can go from 0–60 in an estimated 3secs; it has a potentially record-breaking top speed of over 250mph; it features the biggest rear tyres ever fitted on a production car; it has four wheel drive of course; oh, and it's going to cost in excess of 1,000,000 Euros/US$1,000,000 to get your hands on one. In fact, everything about this supercar is big–the DSG gearbox even has 7 gears to make the most of (and more importantly, tame) the Veyron's amazing W16, 64v quad-turbo 8-liter engine.

VW are adamant that they also want the Veyron to be utterly driveable and not simply a car that sees the bare minimum of miles before being locked up in a high security garage with 24-hour surveillance (though the latter is recommended). And VW want the Veyron to be reliable–just under a dozen of them have already been put through the punishing testing that all VWs, from Lupos upwards, have to go through before they head out to the showroom.

If the word supercar ever seemed too under whelming to describe something as monumental as the Bugatti Veyron, then hypercar would probably do it justice. But only just, mind you.

Copyright Bugatti Automobiles S.A.S.

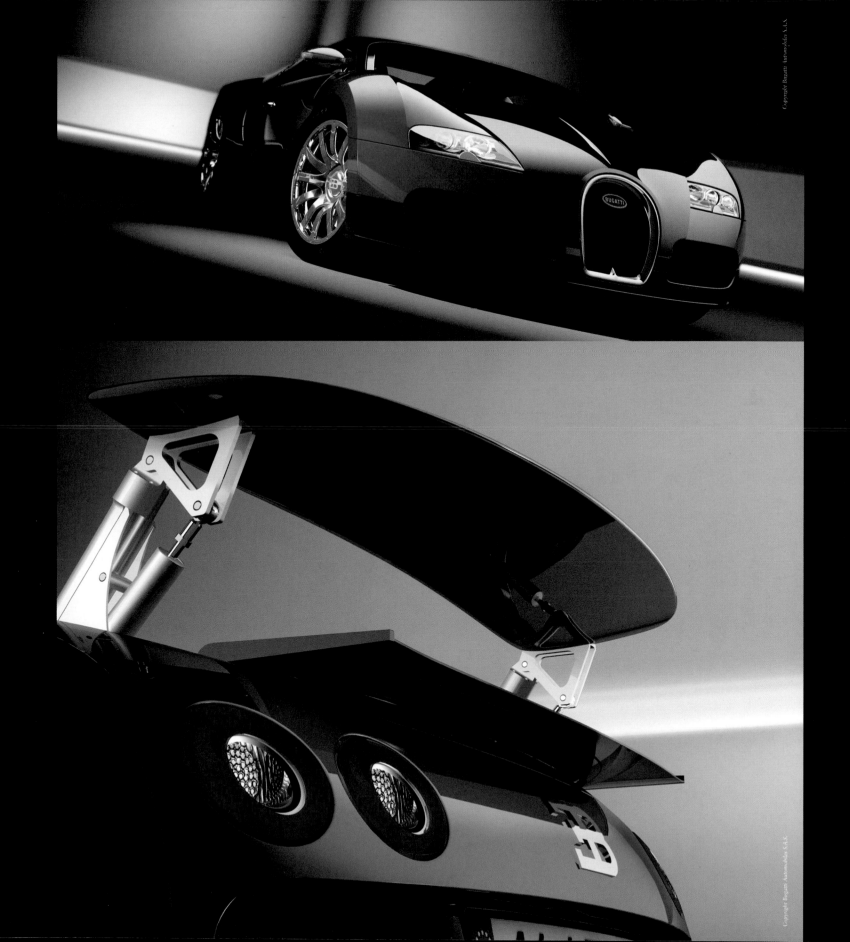

"The Bugatti Veyron could potentially rip asunder every supercar that's gone before it"

Tall Order?

Volkswagen intends to make between 30 to 50 Veyrons a year depending on the demand from customers. And if you're wondering if Volkswagen is actually up to the job of selling supercars, bear in mind that they own Audi–the company that oversaw the creation of the next generation of Lamborghinis.

Back To Its Roots

The Veyron is being assembled at a workshop right next to Chateau St Jean near Mosheim in France–which is the region where the company's founder, Ettore Bugatti, began making his dream cars nearly 100 years ago.

Brake Neck Speeds

With nearly 1,000bhp to propel the driver towards the horizon, it's fairly important that the Veyron can stop as quickly as it can start. To aid in avoiding near disaster when a car pulls out in front of you while you're doing 200mph + on a German autobahn, the Veyron is fitted with specialist carbon-ceramic brakes and a rear wing that can be deployed as an air brake. It is claimed that slamming on the anchors at 248mph will bring the Veyron to a complete standstill in less than 10secs.

Egg-Face Interface

The car's difficult 'gestation period' has been tough for Bugatti–first, a mule version of the car managed to crash at over 200mph. Then the Veyron made an appearance at California's Laguna race track, USA, last year, only to spin off the track and come to a rest in a gravel trap, missing a concrete wall by inches. Much media mirth ensued, but with the progress Bugatti have made, they seem on course to have the last laugh.

Bugatti Veyron (specifications subject to change)

Engine	64v quad turbo W16	Maximum Torque	922lb ft at 2,200-5,500rpm	Kerb Weight	1950kg/4299lbs approx.	Wheels Front	9.5 x 20in
Valvetrain	DOHC 4 Valves / Cyl	Transmission	Seven-speed DSG	Length	4380mm/172in	Wheel Rear	13 x 21in
Displacement	7993cc	0–60mph	3.0secs	Width	1994mm/78in	Price	1,000,000 Euros approx US$1,000,000 approx.
Maximum Power	987bhp at 6,000rpm	Maximum Speed	252mph	Height	1206mm/47in		

Supercars on a Budget

Save winning the lottery, it's inevitable that the intoxicating delights of owning a Lamborghini or a Pagani are well out of the reach of most us; for now, at least. But there's no reason to despair (or seriously consider a career in armed robbery) because there are cars out there that can offer similar thrills to the supercar, but for a fraction of the price.

We're featuring four candidates for your deliberation here that cover a lot of the 'supercar bases' such as great (or outlandish) looks, thrilling performances and handling that delights at every corner. And if none of these suit your budget, take solace in the fact that a quick flick through those local classifieds for secondhand cars will reveal some real driving gems. Think Mazda RX-7 or Subaru Impreza Turbo to name but two of the classics available that guarantee maximum fun for minimal money. After all, there's something for everybody to live out those driving dreams. We'll see you on the road…

No, it's not your typical looking supercar but hey, the British aren't known for settling for the same old, same old...

No windshield, no doors, no headlamps–if you're looking for a luxurious GT capable of crushing continents in a single afternoon, while seating the driver in the lap of luxury, then really the Atom isn't for you. But if you want to bag yourself a sports car that can outrun most supercars on the track and the road when it comes to performance and handling, then the Atom is as good as it gets.

Copyright Ariel Motor Company Ltd

Ariel Atom 2

Perhaps the Atom is the antithesis to the supercar scene's sometimes po-facedness. With no swish bodywork covering up its ultra-lightweight chassis, everything is out on display. Perhaps this is a road-going car that can truly be said to be a perfect example of form following function. And the great thing about the Atom is that its function is so simple–to make you remember why you fell in love with driving in the first place.

And it would be hard not to fall head over heels all over again with the Atom's chassis constantly offering up reams of communication, and the suspension based on one-seater racing cars that can easily be tweaked for track or road use; the Atom can be thrown around corners with abandon. The car's unique composite twin seat unit means that you won't find yourself (or your passenger) being thrown all over the cockpit. Well, it's hardly even a cockpit–there are no frills here, merely the basics required to get started.

As for the Atom's performance on the straight stuff, you can see why the car has gone down a storm–the Ariel Atom 2 released in 2003 offers up the perfect performance to help induce that feel-good factor–after all, it features one of world's finest budget engines (and six-speed gear-boxes) whipped straight out of a Japanese-spec Honda Civic Type R, which produces 220bhp. But bear in mind that the Atom weighs only 456kg/1005lbs–with such a lean kerb weight, it makes the likes of Zonda and Enzo look in need of a two-week stint on a 'fat farm'. And just to rub the salt into those supercar wounds, Ariel offers the Atom in an 'enhanced' supercharged version boasting an insane 300bhp.

This piece of motoring magic is assembled at Ariel's headquarters in Norfolk, UK–'head-quarters' being seven people led by Simon Saunders, a former designer at Aston Martin and GM. It's clear that the Ariel Atom is a labour of love hand-assembled by a group of dedicated enthusiasts. Helmet recommended.

"*The Ariel Atom 2 features one of the world's finest budget engines whipped straight out of a Japanese-spec Honda Civic Type R*"

Ariel Atom 2: The Specifications

Engine	Honda iVTEC / 4 Cyl	Maximum torque	145lb ft at 6,100rpm	Maximum speed	135mph
Displacement	1998cc	Transmission	Six-speed manual	Kerb weight	456kg
Maximum power	220bhp at 8,200rpm	0-60 mph	3.5secs	Price	£26,000
					US price not available

The miracle makers based in Norfolk, UK, first launched the Lotus Exige in 2000; the mid-engine coupé was actually based on the Mk I Lotus Elise, the firm's critically acclaimed two-seater roadster. In 2004 though, the Exige was relaunched this time featuring a Toyota 1.8-liter VVT-i engine instead of the original's Rover K-series. The reason? So Lotus could start selling the Exige in the USA–after all, that Toyota engine passes all the US's strict emissions regulations whereas the K-series never did. The bullet-proof Toyota engine generates 189bhp which makes the Exige zip from 0-60 in 4.9secs.

Offering outstanding performance on the track, and the ability to be an everyday runabout, the Exige is also packed with racing pedigree...

Lotus Exige

The key as to why the Exige can deliver quite such neck-snapping acceleration from this un-supercar-like lump is thanks to the car's light weight. The Exige's underpinnings are now based on the Elise Mk II–in fact, the extruded and bonded aluminum tub, with a steel rear subframe, is used in the Elise 111R. Lotus though have used stiffer springs and dampers on the Exige to ensure that the driver can make the most of the car's performance and to ensure that body roll is kept to a minimum.

The Exige with its roof scoop, fast back roof and rear wing certainly fulfils Lotus's desire to produce a race car for the road–and it delivers on all its visual drama. Renowned for its communicative chassis, body control and non-power assisted tactile steering, the Exige wasn't born to scare the hell out of you but just to offer the driver an adrenaline rush every time they pressed down on the accelerator.

And with its supreme aerodynamic package, the race car feels nailed to the road with enough downforce being provided no matter how fast you're going. Couple that with its specially designed tyres and no corner is too sharp or scary for the Exige. The question isn't whether the car can take it; the real question is–can you?

The car highlighted on these pages is the specially commissioned Lotus Exige Sport that features carbon fiber bodywork and front splitter, a rear diffuser, and an adjustable rear wing for added downforce. Instead of the Toyota engine, there's a 400bhp 3-liter V6 lump paired with a sequential six-speed gearbox. Unfortunately, the car that took only six months to develop is a one-off that was ordered by a client who is expected to use the Exige Sport in Asian racing.

Customers wanting a more extreme version of the standard Exige will have to make do with Exige Sport 240R which features 240hp and a supercar-crushing 0-60 in 3.9secs–do bear in mind though that only 50 will ever see the light of day. So best to get that order in now.

"No corner is too sharp or scary for the Exige. The question isn't whether the car can take it; the real question is can you?"

Lotus Exige: The Specifications

Engine	Aluminum Inline-4
Displacement	1796cc
Maximum power	189bhp at 7,800rpm
Maximum torque	133.5lb ft at 6,800rpm
Transmission	Six-speed manual
0-60 mph	4.9secs
0-100 mph	13.2secs
Maximum speed	147mph
Kerb weight	875kg/1929lbs
Price	£29,995 US$50–55,000 estimated

'Luxury and performance' all wrapped up in mini-supercar looks. The SLK350 is one very special car...

Mercedes-Benz SLK350

The original SLK was a great car–for posers. Its main party trick was the ability to turn from a coupé into an open-top roadster in seconds thanks to its smart metal retractable roof. The trouble was, for all its sporty pretensions, it could never match the might of the sublime Porsche Boxster. Enter the SLK MkII; everything about the roadster is infinitely better–this is no poser's car that is destined to be parked outside fancy wine bars or driven by hair stylists. The SLK is actually now a proper sports car that the diehard enthusiast wouldn't be embarrassed to be seen in.

It's those looks–the original SLK may have been a smart if slightly effeminate design, but the SLK MkII is far more like a muscular roadster thanks to its F1-style nose 'inspired' by its (very) big brother, the SLR. The folding metal roof remains and is now more of an elegant design–and more importantly, it goes up quickly in case rain interrupts play.

The entry model SLK200 powered by a supercharged 1.8-liter is best suited to those who want more show than go. It provides adequate performance for a droptop–0-60 in 8.3secs–but hardly the kind of acceleration that will trouble a sporty family sedan, never mind a full-blooded supercar with a V12. No, the model to aim for is the rather fine SLK350.

Featuring a warbling 3.5-liter V6, the torque-happy engine offers plenty of power for the thrillseeker. On the road, the little Benz feels planted, tackling corners with the kind of hunger that the original sorely lacked. You also feel safe; perhaps too safe for some–the ESP has been criticized for taking the fun out of the SLK even when switched off (it isn't really ever 'off'–it's always there in the background monitoring). But for the everyday driver, there's more than enough entertainment on offer to make that grin creep higher towards their ears.

Thankfully, the SLK also now has a quality six-speed gearbox as standard for the driver who likes to feel absolutely in control of that V6 in front of him–while the SLK MkI eventually did have a manual option, it was quite frankly naff. For those who want a more leisurely life, the SLK features Mercedes' unique seven-speed auto–in manual mode, it's accessible through the buttons mounted on the steering wheel. Mercedes claims that the auto shaves 0.1secs off the 0-60 time. Whether it shaves some of the fun off too is open to debate.

For those supercar aficionados who are still not convinced, there is the option of upping the budget and splashing out on the £47,730/$60,500 (approx) SLK55 AMG that features a 5.5-liter V8 engine producing a very healthy 360bhp and a 0-60 time of 4.9secs. Surely that's enough power for those who can't stretch to a supercar three times the price?

Most of us though will be happy with the SLK350. It's a near-perfect blend–a bruiser when you're in the mood and an extremely comfortable cruiser when you're not.

"The SLK350 is a near-perfect blend; a bruiser when you're in the mood and an extremely comfortable cruiser when you're not"

Mercedes-Benz SLK350: The Specifications

Engine	V6
Displacement	3498cc
Maximum power	272bhp at 6,000rpm
Maximum torque	258lb ft at 2,400rpm
Transmission	Six-speed manual/Seven-speed auto
0-60 mph	5.6secs
Maximum speed	155mph
Kerb weight	1465kg/3231lbs
Price	£34,270/US$46,220

Picture the scene–you've just spent a fortune on an Italian supercar; the cost doesn't matter because you're know you're in something special–that pedigree, those looks... and the bespoke leather luggage. Out on the open road, you decide to floor the accelerator for the first time. And as you roar off–your ego swelling to the size of a small African state–a car that costs a tenth of what you paid for yours overtakes you.

Supercar performance, but at a fraction of the price. Discover the small car guaranteed to deliver big grins...

'Ouch' is the only word that will suffice because you've just been 'VX'd'. Welcome to the rather brilliant Vauxhall VX220 Turbo. It's all the more remarkable if you consider the car's manufacturer –Vauxhall (owned by General Motors), in the UK, has been perceived for decades as a rather run-of-the-mill car manufacturer. They've made perfectly good family cars, sedans, MPVS and so on, but Vauxhall always seemed like a car maker that lacked a certain spark–they lacked excitement.

VX220 is actually a 're-skinned' Elise, but Vauxhall insisted that only 141 parts were shared with its equally illustrious brother. The Lotus-built VX is also acknowledged to be more forgiving for the over-eager driver than the Elise–and it is all the better for it.

Vauxhall VX220 Turbo

So creating excitement became the job of the original VX220 launched in 2000. On the face of it, Vauxhall should have struggled to produce such a fantastic two-seater roadster but they had help–they went to Lotus. The rear-engined

Featuring an aluminum chassis and plastic body panels, the original VX220 had a 2.2-liter engine that could do 0-60 in 5.6secs. But that wasn't powerful enough for Vauxhall... so they released the VX220 Turbo. Featuring 197bhp from the 2-liter turbo engine, the car can now make the sprint from 0-60 in a mere 4.7secs–that's Vanquish S country–and it has a top speed of 151mph, which is more than enough for a public road. The handling of the VX is superb as well–flat and taut with large dollops of information being fed back to the driver about what is going on under the tyres. This may be a serious driver's car, but treat it with the respect it deserves, and it's also real controllable fun.

In 2004, Vauxhall released an even hotter version of the VX, the VXR220, which could hit 0-60 in only 4.2secs and only ran out of puff at 154mph. Alas, due to its limited production number of 65 cars, they all sold out in six weeks–typical supercar then.

Luxury lovers may find the VX's interiors somewhat spartan–there are precious few toys and those hoping to find mod cons as simple as electric windows have to make do with manual winders. But such omissions are there for one very good reason–to keep the pocket rocket's weight down. The VX also features a canvas roof that can be rolled off and stored in the tiny 'trunk' with relative ease. All in all, the little Vauxhall is a car that offers the thrills of supercar ownership without the costs.

*"Vauxhall should have
struggled to produce such
a fantastic two-seater
roadster but they had help...
they went to Lotus"*

Vauxhall VX220 Turbo:
The Specifications

Engine	Iline-4
Displacement	1998cc
Maximum power	197bhp at 5,500rpm
Maximum torque	184lb ft from 1,950rpm
Transmission	Six-speed manual
0-60 mph	4.7secs
0-100 mph	Under 13secs
Maximum speed	151mph
Kerb weight	930kg/2050lbs
Price	£25,495/Not available in US